Decanates

Bernice Prill Grebner

ISBN-10: 0-86690-109-4
ISBN-13: 978-0-86690-109-3

Cover Design: Jack Cipolla

Published by:
American Federation of Astrologers, Inc.
6535 S. Rural Road
Tempe, AZ 85283

www.astrologers.com

Printed in the United States of America

Dedicated to the eternal Sweet Prince!

Contents

Introduction

Whenever you consider any interpretation in astrology, heritage and environment play a very important role in the character of the individual. The charts of parents, brothers, sisters, grandparents, and even close friends, are important in relationship to the chart of the individual being interpreted. The local chart of the city or area where the individual lives is also a consideration if a more perfect analysis is to be computed. This indicates whether relationships to family and environment are favorable or unfavorable.

The sign itself is the projector; the decanate is the receiver. The dwad—the 2½-degree division of the decanate—shows the daily experiences that may help the development of the sign, which is the ultimate goal. The house position (how) shows the conditions the individual is involved in to bring this about. The decanate shows the where, in what, and for what.

Consider the example of an Aries Sun in the Leo decanate. Here we have pioneering leadership, with the energy falling into the decanate's co-ruler, Leo; this is where leadership is best served or completed. This influence would be dramatics, children, creative love, self-expression, or excessive fun and games.

An Aries Sun in the Sagittarius decanate indicates pioneering leadership best served in philosophy, religion, or higher education, or through travel.

An Aries Moon in the Sagittarius decanate, Capricorn dwad, and the sixth house indicates the emotional nature is released, soothed, and made stronger when projected through philosophy, religious leadership, Capricorn-type daily experiences or associations with Capricorn individuals who help to control the Aries emotional nature, work, service to others, improvement of health conditions, or the study of nutrition. The dwads and house conditions indicate what is necessary in order to achieve the best constructive use of the sign and planet.

All the aspects to a Sun sign or planet are like connecting wires that dilute or strengthen, according to the specific aspect. For example, the square acts as an impetus that pushes one forward or into that over which the individual has little control. In some cases the square may indicate a lack of confidence, so he or she exerts more effort to compensate.

A Pisces Moon in the Scorpio decanate in a man's chart represents a Pisces- or Scorpio-oriented woman in his life, his emotional nature, and his relationship with women in general. Pisces represents karma, self-sacrifice, or the ability to rise to spiritual love. The Pisces influence is projected into Scorpio, which can be sex or the partner's money. In other words, it is through sexual experiences and/or money that he will learn his lesson and come to a more spiritual, self-sacrificing emotional nature. The Scorpio dwad would indicate learning experiences in daily life, or mysterious, hidden occurrences in connection with his emotional life, or with a woman. If it is a third house position, conditions in the environment may help or hinder, travel may be necessary, or there may be a need to learn to communicate more easily.

When interpreting your chart, take a broad view and think about what you want to do and then why it must be done and how you are going to do it. What are the daily or mundane conditions necessary to complete your goal?

Chapter 1

Decanates and Dwads

A decanate is 10 degrees of a sign, with each sign being divided into three parts, for a total of 30 degrees. The first decanate (0-10°) represents the physical influence; the second decanate (10-20°) represents the mental influence; and the third decanate (20-30°) represents the spiritual influence. When interpreting the physical (first decanate) of any sign, always consider Mars by sign and house in the chart in relationship to the particular planet in this first decanate. (Also consider the influence of Pluto, the transformer.) The mental (second decanate) relates to Mercury and its house placement in relationship to the planet in this second decanate. (Also consider the influence of Uranus, the enlightener.) The spiritual (third decanate) focus on Saturn and Jupiter in the chart to complete the influence in order to discover how the spiritual (Jupiter) will be carried out and where (Saturn), and where the test will come and how.

The decanate is then further divided into four parts called dwads, each of which is two and a half degrees. These tools can be used to interpret and analyze everything in the chart, from the most minute detail to the overall view. We need first to look at the broad view in order to see where we are going.

The decanate represents the individual's purpose, and the dwad tells the approach or conditions that will influence the individual and in what element problems are dealt with. Listed below are the decanates and their divisions into dwads. The listing also shows each dwad's element. It is this difference in element between the sign and the decanate that gives the key.

Aries: Leadership, Fire

First Decanate 0-10°, Aries-Aries; physical; fire, enthusiasm
    0-2½°, Aries dwad, fire, enthusiastic and impulsive energy
    2½-5°, Taurus dwad, earth, practical energy
    5-7½°, Gemini dwad, air, mental stimulation (into action in the environment)
    7½-10°, Cancer dwad, air, emotional exhilaration (into action in the home)

Second Decanate 10-20°, Aries-Leo; mental; fire; optimism
    10-12½°, Leo dwad, fire, energy used creatively through love
    12½-15°, Virgo dwad, earth, energy used in a methodical manner
    15-17½°, Libra dwad, air, energy dependent upon a partner to be at best
    17½-20°, Scorpio dwad, water, energy that has a self-rejuvenating outlet

Third Decanate 20-30°, Aries-Sagittarius; spiritual; fire; inspiration
    20-22½°, Sagittarius dwad, fire, energy used to pursue higher truth
    22½-25°, Capricorn dwad, earth, energy disciplined into leadership
    25-27½°, Aquarius dwad, air, energy for progressive causes
    27½-30°, Pisces dwad, water, psychic energy used to inspire others

Taurus: Material or Values, Earth

First Decanate 0-10°, Taurus-Taurus; physical; earth; practical
    0-2½°, Taurus dwad, earth, stubborn practicality, unbendable determination
    2½-5°, Gemini dwad, air, practicality that can be reasoned through a mental outlook
    5-7½°, Cancer dwad, water, practicality that has an emotional influence
    7½-10°, Leo dwad, fire, creative talent, materially productive

Second Decanate 10-20°, Taurus Virgo; mental; earth; logical
    10-12½°, Virgo dwad, earth, critical and detail-oriented logic
    12½-15°, Libra dwad, air, logic that is persuasive and fair
    15½-17°, Scorpio dwad, water, logic that must have purpose behind it
    17½-20°, Sagittarius dwad, fire, inspiration must come before logic

Third Decanate, 20-30°, Taurus-Capricorn; spiritual; earth; realistic and responsible
    20-22½°, Capricorn dwad, earth, ambitious practicality, materialistic, income
    22½-25°, Aquarius dwad, air, innovations that are realistic
    25-27½°, Pisces dwad, water, idealism that can be practical
    27½-30°, Aries dwad, fire, practical nature with leadership

Gemini: Mental, Air

First Decanate, 0-10°, Gemini-Gemini; physical; air; inquisitive mind
    0-2½°, Gemini dwad, air, inquisitive communication
    2½-5o, Cancer dwad, water, emotional communication
    5-7½°, Leo dwad, fire, pleasurable or dramatic communication
    7½-10°, Virgo dwad, earth, analytical or detailed communication

Second Decanate, 10-20°, Gemini-Libra; air; persuasive mind
    10-12½°, Libra dwad, air, sociable, diplomatic communication
    12½-15°, Scorpio dwad, water, subtle communication, mystery or secrecy)
    15-17½°, Sagittarius dwad, fire, inspirational communication or understanding
    17½-20°, Capricorn dwad, earth, reserved or useful communication (sometimes patronizing)

Third Decanate, 20-30°, Gemini-Aquarius; air, progressive mind
    20-22½°, Aquarius dwad, air, communication with friends
    22½-25°, Pisces dwad, water, psychic communication (or music and poetry)
    25-27½°, Aries dwad, fire, communicating ideas of a progressive nature
    27½-30°, Taurus dwad, earth, acute sensuous communication (or talk about money)

Cancer: Emotions, Water

First Decanate, 0-10°, Cancer-Cancer, physical, water, feeling
    0-2½°, Cancer dwad, water, protective feelings or the need to be nurtured
    2½-5°, Leo dwad, fire, pleasurable feelings or the need for dramatics in some form
    5-7½°, Virgo dwad, earth, discriminating feelings or need to be of service
    7½-10°, Libra dwad, air, indecisive feelings or need to be fair

Second Decanate, 10-20°, Cancer-Scorpio, mental, water, heroic or suspicious
    10-12½°, Scorpio dwad, water, heroic tendencies or emotions
    12½-15°, Sagittarius dwad, fire, inspirational emotions
    15-17½°, Capricorn dwad, earth, ambitious feelings, suspicious in nature
    17½-20°, Aquarius dwad, air, detached feelings for family

Third Decanate, 20-30°, Cancer-Pisces, spiritual, water, psychic
    20-22½°, Pisces dwad, water, sensitivity to unseen vibrations
    22½-25°, Aries dwad, fire, leadership in psychic research
    25-27½°, Taurus dwad, earth, acute sensory perception in psychic talent
    27½-30°, Gemini dwad, air, sensitivity to environmental intuition

Leo: Dramatic Talent, Personal Love, Fire

First Decanate, 0-10°, Leo-Leo, physical, fire, in love with love

  0-2½°, Leo dwad, fire, dramatic display of love or love of dramatic arts

  2½-5°, Virgo dwad, earth, perfected love or love of perfection

  5-7½°, Libra dwad, air, love that is strongly partner influenced

  7½-10°, Scorpio dwad, water, secret love or love until death

Second Decanate, 10-20°, Leo-Sagittarius, mental, fire, high-minded love

  10-12½°, Sagittarius dwad, fire, love with freedom to be objective

  12½-15°, Capricorn dwad, earth, ambitious love or love inspiring high ambitions

  15-17½°, Aquarius dwad, air, unusual love, progressive movements

  17½-20°, Pisces dwad, water, sacrificial love leading to greater spirituality

Third Decanate, 20-30°, Leo-Aries, spiritual, fire, self-love

  20-22½°, Aries dwad, fire, leadership in drama or leading role in love

  22½-25°, Taurus dwad, earth, love subject to financial influence

  25-27½°, Gemini dwad, air, love expression that can lead to creative writing

  27½-30°, Cancer dwad, water, protective love or love of children

Virgo: Service and Discrimination, Earth

First Decanate 0-10°, Virgo-Virgo, physical, earth, capable of detail work, great discrimination

  0-2½°, Virgo dwad, earth, humble service to others

  2½-5°, Libra dwad, air, judicious service to others

  5-7½°, Scorpio dwad, water, capable of a great capacity for work that has a purpose

  7½-10°, Sagittarius dwad, fire, enthusiastic, objective service

Second Decanate, 10-20°, Virgo-Capricorn, mental, earth, combining work and ambition

  10-12½°, Capricorn dwad, earth, successful service

  12½-15°, Aquarius dwad, air, political service

  15-17½°, Pisces dwad, water, healing profession or service to all

  17½-20°, Aries dwad, fire, enterprising, ambitious leadership that pioneers in a service

Third Decanate, 20-30°, Virgo-Taurus, spiritual, earth, ambition to acquire resources

  20-22½°, Taurus dwad, earth, money-oriented or value conscious

  22½-25°, Gemini dwad, air, money and ambition acquired through communication

  25-27½°, Cancer dwad, water, tenacity builds resources

  27½-30°, Leo dwad, fire, money and success through creativity

Libra: Harmony, Fairness, Dependence, Air

First Decanate, 0-10°, Libra-Libra, physical, air, dependence
  0-2½°, Libra dwad, air, affectionate dependence upon another
  2½-5°, Scorpio dwad, water, financial or sexual dependence upon another
  5-7½°, Sagittarius dwad, fire, intellectual stimulus needed from another
  7½-10°, Capricorn dwad, earth, business partnership or protective mate

Second Decanate, 10-20o, Libra-Aquarius, mental, air, fairness
  10-12½°, Aquarius dwad, air, broad-minded relationships
  12½-15°, Pisces dwad, water, compassion in relating or sacrifice for partner
  15-17½°, Aries dwad, fire, action involved with a mate or leadership inspired by a mate
  17½-20°, Taurus dwad, earth, materialistic partnership not easily broken or mate is one's value

Third Decanate, 20-30°, Libra-Gemini, spiritual, air, harmony in environment or with siblings
  20-22½°, Gemini dwad, air, public relations or artistic expression
  22½-25°, Cancer dwad, water, family harmony important
  25-27½°, Leo dwad, fire, love and marriage or harmony in love
  27½-30°, Virgo dwad, earth, seeking mental harmony in relationships or the perfect partner

Scorpio: Magnetic, Secretive, Penetrating, Water

First Decanate, 0-10°, Scorpio-Scorpio, physical, water, heroic
  0-2½°, Scorpio dwad, water, mysterious, secretly heroic
  2½o-5°, Sagittarius dwad, fire, a religious hero
  5-7½°, Capricorn dwad, earth, a financier who becomes a hero because of his or her position
  7½-10°, Aquarius dwad, air, the crusader for human rights

Second Decanate, 10-20°, Scorpio-Pisces, mental, water, healing
  10-12½°, Pisces dwad, water, a natural healer
  12½-15°, Aries dwad, fire, a leader in a healing field or capable of pioneering a new method
  15-17½°, Taurus dwad, earth, material success in the healing field or sensuous passion
  17½-20°, Gemini dwad, air, mystery to others in the environment or a writer/reader of mysteries

Third Decanate, 20-30°, Scorpio-Cancer, spiritual, water, tenacious
  20-22½°, Cancer dwad, water, extremely conscious of security
  22½-25°, Leo dwad, fire, intensity of emotional nature, ability to combine love and passion
  25-27½°, Virgo dwad, earth, a person capable of deep, analytical research
  27½-30°, Libra dwad, air, a deep and abiding partner, but perhaps jealous

Sagittarius: Religion, Philosophy, Freedom, Fire

First Decanate, 0-10°, Sagittarius-Sagittarius, physical, fire, lover of freedom
    0-2½°, Sagittarius dwad, fire, a broad view of life or objective interpretation
    2½-5°, Capricorn dwad, earth, religious attainment or discipline
    5-7½°, Aquarius dwad, air, humanitarian philosophy, belief in freedom for all people
    7½-10°, Pisces dwad, water, very spiritual to the point of sacrifice

Second Decanate, 10-20°, Sagittarius-Aries, mental, fire, intellectual and religious pioneering
    10-12½°, Aries dwad, fire, intellectual ideas in religion or philosophy
    12½-15°, Taurus dwad, earth, construction of or establishing a place of learning or worship
    15-17½°, Gemini dwad, air, bringing learned truths to others
    17½-20°, Cancer dwad, water, historian who can be an authority in a specific field

Third Decanate, 20-30°, Sagittarius-Leo, spiritual, fire, intellectual or religious domination
    20-22½°, Leo dwad, fire, religious optimism or love of religious ritual
    22½-25°, Virgo dwad, earth, working tirelessly for a cause and a critic
    25-27½°, Libra dwad, air, strong belief in supreme justice
    27½-30°, Scorpio dwad, water, mystical and religious research

Capricorn: Ambition, Thrift, Responsibility, Discipline, Earth

First Decanate, 0-10°, Capricorn-Capricorn, physical, earth, ambition, success
    0-2½°, Capricorn dwad, earth, attainment through effort and duty
    2½-5°, Aquarius dwad, air, original type of ambition
    5-7½°, Pisces dwad, water, dual form of direction or ambition starting with idealism
    7½-10°, Aries dwad, fire, business leadership or pioneering a new type of business

Second Decanate, 10-20°, Capricorn-Taurus, mental, earth, thrift, accumulation
    10-12½°, Taurus dwad, earth, financial know-how and accumulation
    12½-15°, Gemini dwad, air, business success involving communication
    15-17½°, Cancer dwad, water, instinct for knowing public need and capitalizing on it
    17½-20°, Leo dwad, fire, success in the entertainment field or with young people

Third Decanate, 20-30°, Capricorn-Virgo, spiritual, earth, methodical and cautious worker
    20-22½°, Virgo dwad, earth, a trouble-shooter capable of finding and correcting mistakes
    22½-25°, Libra dwad, air, diplomacy that can lead to patronizing behavior
    25-27½°, Scorpio dwad, water, instinctive financial knowledge gives success with resources
    27½-30°, Sagittarius dwad, fire, a broad view that helps encourage overall success

Aquarius: Impersonal, Unconventional, Progressive, Air

First Decanate, 0-10°, Aquarius-Aquarius, physical, air, progressive
    0-2½°, Aquarius dwad, air, very progressive and ahead of the times
    2½-5°, Pisces dwad, water, compassionate and people oriented
    5-7½°, Aries dwad, fire, a leader or idea person in causes or groups
    7½-10°, Taurus dwad, earth, resistant to progressive ideas or earnings in humanitarian causes

Second Decanate, 10-20°, Aquarius-Gemini, mental, air, communicator of progress
    10-12½°, Gemini dwad, air, writer and speaker of advanced ideas
    12½-15°, Cancer dwad, water, ability to appeal to public and to present advanced ideas
    15-17½°, Leo dwad, fire, oriented to deal with children progressively to bring out uniqueness
    17½-20°, Virgo dwad, earth, ability to work tirelessly with humanity

Third Decanate, 20-30°, Aquarius-Libra, spiritual, air, impersonal relationships
    20-22½°, Libra dwad, air, fairness to all and impersonal judgment
    22½-25°, Scorpio dwad, water, ultimate belief in a cause
    25-27½°, Sagittarius dwad, fire, a philosopher of human affairs
    27½-30°, Capricorn dwad, earth, tempering realism with advanced ideas and executing them

Pisces: Sympathetic, Martyrdom, Gentleness, Compassion, Water

First Decanate, 0-10°, Pisces-Pisces, physical, water, sensitive awareness
    0-2½°, Pisces dwad, water, mystical and compassionate
    2½-5°, Aries dwad, fire, much self-sacrificing
    5-7½°, Taurus dwad, earth, extremely impressionable through the senses
    7½-10°, Gemini dwad, air, sensitive to surroundings and acutely aware of environment

Second Decanate, 10-20°, Pisces-Cancer, mental, water, sympathetic
    10-12½°, Cancer dwad, water, absorbs the hurts of others
    12½-15°, Leo dwad, fire, gentle and loving with children
    15-17½°, Virgo dwad, earth, interested in healing the ill
    17½-20°, Libra dwad, air, peacemaker

Third Decanate, 20-30°, Pisces-Scorpio, spiritual, water, martyrdom
    20-22½°, Scorpio dwad, water, capable of great martyrdom or negative self-destruction
    22½-25°, Sagittarius dwad, fire, extremely idealistic and capable of noble sacrifice
    25-27½°, Capricorn dwad, earth, compassionate strength and protection
    27½-30°, Aquarius dwad, air, my brother's keeper;

Chapter 2

Planetary Interpretations

When interpreting each decanate in the chart, always consider the location of the sign ruler and the ruler of the decanate and its house position in order to show by what and how the decanate development will be fulfilled or completed. For example, with the Sagittarius decanate of Aries, look to Jupiter's placement and the house with Sagittarius on the cusp. Although the following descriptions apply primarily to the Sun, they can be adapted for the other planets.

Aries-Aries, The Pioneer: First Decanate, 0-10°, Mars-Mars, Physical

These are the true pioneers, fearless individuals who are strongly self-sufficient as this Mars-Mars combination relates to the Sun (ego). To be true to the destiny this placement offers, these people must initiate something that has not been done before, or at least be willing and able to proceed with life in an individual manner while really getting to know the self. Aries is not the imitator but the person who is imitated. People with this decanate have an abundance of energy that is strictly physical in its influence, but if it is not used wisely and constructively, power and talent can turn toward useless recklessness. Aries then becomes the daredevil. As this first decanate of Aries is co-ruled by Aries (Mars), the keyword is *action*, and the head is the physical relationship. These are the idea people and thus they are compelled to begin an activity, which usually isn't finished. Because there is so much accent on self, Aries can become egotistical and self-centered and dislikes being told what to do. A negative trait is the inability to understand others. They will not get the affection they want until they listen to others and try to under-

9

stand the other fellow's point of view. They also must learn to be alone or to do things by themselves. Therefore, this person can be a *loner*. It depends upon aspects to this Aries-Aries Sun how the leadership quality will manifest. Naturally, the house position will make the difference, but this is *how*. The *why* should be taken into consideration through the aspects. Look to Mars by sign and house for the action.

Need: To really get to know themselves and where their uniqueness can lead others.

Aries-Leo, The Gambler: Second Decanate, 10-20°, Mars-Sun, Mental

The keyword with this decanate is *intensity*. This section of Aries-Leo is more magnanimous and loving, less self-centered and more domineering. They combine romance with adventure, giving them an exciting life, and have more staying power and a tendency to be dramatic. This decanate gives an abundance of creative energy. This Aries-Leo can talk you into anything, for the talent here lies in mental communication. The energy (Mars) must have a creative outlet to be at its best; otherwise, it takes the form of drama in relationships or in self-aggrandizement. The negative form of this is the power-hungry leader or one who is too much a lover of fun and games. This too can show excessive ego and much more than Aries-Aries in the way of affectation. Aries-Aries people care mainly about what they as individuals are doing and rarely care about influencing others. The Aries-Leo ego, however, must have an outlet, and the position of the Sun shows where it can be best served. This is similar to a Sun-Mars conjunction in that it gives a lot of drive, energy and self-confidence. Negatively, it can be used for ego stimulation to hold power over others. The person must find a balance between energy and ego. This is the idea person in the creative arts. Whatever his or her ambition is in life, it is fed by noble affection.

Need: To use the energy for creative accomplishments rather than ego stimulation.

Aries-Sagittarius, The Hero: Third Decanate, 20-30°, Mars-Jupiter, Spiritual

The keyword for this decanate is *circulate* (good or bad, depending upon the aspects to it). These are the leaders in philosophical or religious discussions and the champions of the weak. Collectors and dispensers of information, they are sometimes too forceful in expression and need to be more tactful. They are leaders in education and also fearless adventurers, and people with this position have big ideas. Enthusiasm, however, may be short-lived. The ruler of this decanate is Jupiter, so where Jupiter is located by sign and house and its relationship to Mars is vastly important to the outlet of this ego-based Sun sign and house position. This decanate has the same effect as Mars conjunct Jupiter, so there can be excess energy and over-indulgence, especially in the sexual area, or an excess of the adventurous spirit. Religion, higher education, philosophy, and educating by writing or publishing are the positive higher vibrations of this position, especially if there is a trine of Jupiter to this decanate or to the Sun. They believe in truth and are the most outspoken of the Aries decanates. A square to Jupiter or the Sun's decanate gives an enthusiastic drive coupled with great energy in the pursuit of these above-mentioned goals. However, the square could also give more impetus for a physical (sexual) outlet. There is a great desire to see the world and to travel. Aries is more interested in using energy in sports and outdoor activities (all decanates).

Need: To use the energy for teaching and directing others in a religious setting or one that involves the higher mind.

Taurus-Taurus, The Singer: First Decanate, 0-10°, Venus-Venus, Physical

The keyword for this decanate of Taurus is *determination*. It gives stability and reliability. You cannot push these people, but you can lead them through love. They can be too timid, thus limiting their advancement in life, and the need here is to use determination. These people are very stubborn and cannot be easily changed, and the senses are very strong and usually in need of control, but a rich, deep voice in speaking or singing is common. The ruler of the decanate is Venus, which by sign and place is the outlet of higher ego activities. The people having this placement are slow and plodding, and usually finish what they start. This decanate gives an orientation to love of beautiful objects and the acquisition of those objects. It is the most possessive combination in the zodiac, and they can become money hungry to the exclusion of all else in life. They are stable and loyal, and devotion once given remains until death. They need to develop some kind of artistic expression.

Need: To control the acute sensuous nature and direct the physical energy to the actual construction of a material object or perfect an artistic expression.

Taurus-Virgo, The Gardener: Second Decanate, 10-20°, Venus-Mercury, Mental

The keyword for this decanate is *struggle*. These people are detailed and dedicated to service. This decanate has more intellectual agility than the other decanates, and is not quite so stubborn, and these people are more flexible than are those of the first or third decanate. People with this placement are fussy, critical, and neat. The co-ruler of this decanate is Mercury, so this planet's placement by sign and house must be considered in addition to the third and sixth houses. Similar to Mercury conjunct Venus, this placement is cooperative and gracious, and the desire for money is blended with the ability to work hard, so they are usually financially successful. This vibration gives the know-how to gain material resources, but slowly because they are steady, dependable workers. The mental focus of this decanate can lead to a clash of wills, but this can be used constructively to attain success in writing or anything involving detailed calculations. These people listen more than those born under other Taurus decanates, and they have a love of refinement and ease of living. They could be orators or be involved with nature.

Need: To overcome physical limitations with mental force that causes obstacles to crumble.

Taurus-Capricorn, The Banker: Third Decanate, 20-30°, Venus-Saturn, Spiritual

The keyword for this decanate is *masterdom*. This vibration represents money and business, and this position can aid success in the business field, primarily because of a stubborn dedication to advancement. It is difficult for Taurus-Capricorn individuals to detach from people, and even if love has lost its radiance and they are unhappy, they will remain faithful. It is not easy for Taurus to let go of either a love or a possession. They are also rather tight with their money, and need to learn to give because they tend to be takers. Here again a positive vibration by aspect from Jupiter or Venus would promote generosity not only with love but money. These people tend to think in terms of black and all white, and need to accept that there is also gray in life. Prestige is very important to them, so they could become patronizing. Those with this decanate are more conventional and serious, and like all the Taurus decanates, they like sweets and pastry. Duty and happiness in relation to loved ones is strong, and this Venus-Saturn combination usually ensures loyalty and trust.

Need: To master and discipline the physical appetite to attain spiritual growth, and to transform stinginess into spiritual giving.

Gemini-Gemini, The Writer: First Decanate, 0-10°, Mercury-Mercury, Physical

The keyword for this decanate is *insight*. These people are the most variable and mentally curious of the zodiac, and also physically restless. There is a strong tie with siblings, and they are neighborly to all and know no strangers. These people are talkative and rarely still and need to learn to be mentally and physically quiet. They need to express themselves in order to be at peace with their world, but they need to learn to listen and to let other people talk. Gemini wants to move about and be on the go, and there is a tendency to skate over the surface of almost everything. The difficulty comes when they are backed into a corner and forced to commit to in-depth involvement. The best job for these people is one that involves travel or a variety of tasks as this will help their restless nature. Their greatest desire is to learn and discover what life is all about, and they know a little about a lot. But they also need to learn to direct more of their mental energy and attention into a single endeavor in order to develop expertise. Their life mission is communication, and they have open minds, but they also need to learn to communicate something of value. Because of restlessness and intense mental activity, however, their energy is more easily drained. So they need to learn to be quiet, relax, and listen to and rely on their intuition. On the physical plane these people have an interest in soul development. Look to the house with Virgo on the cusp to discover the direction from which relaxation can come and where mental processes can be more detailed and focused.

Need: To learn to hear the voice of silence in order to more clearly follow their own insights as too much talk can block their own higher intuition.

Gemini-Libra, The Diplomat: Second Decanate, 10-20°, Mercury-Venus, Mental

The keyword is *faithful*, and this is the decanate of soul mates. This means there is a strong likelihood that these people, more than those born under the other decanates, will find loving mates. This soul mate attraction is also true when this Gemini decanate is on the cusp of the seventh house or if the Sun and Venus are in Libra or the Libra decanate of any other air sign. These people are faithful companions, and often do best in a career dealing with people because they are diplomats. They are fair, but there can be much mental indecision, which delays their destiny and growth. This placement gives artistic and creative talent. Gemini dislikes routine work, and people with this decanate can be the laziest of the three Gemini decanates. Learning to maintain balance is important as this is the conscious expression of Venus vibrations (love, beauty, art). These people delight in seeing all that is beautiful, which is also true of the Libra-Gemini decanate. Because they are so oriented toward sight appreciation and attract this into their lives, they need to learn to express this appreciation to those around them. This expression can take the form of words, works of art, or flowers in or outside their homes. The important thing is that they convey the message of beauty to others. With this Venus-Mercury combination, these people are articulate and refined.

Need: To make decisions and stick to them, to express affection in partnership, and to develop two-way communication.

Gemini-Aquarius, The Lecturer: Third Decanate, 20-30°, Mercury-Uranus, Spiritual

The keyword is *reason*. This gives a scientific or creative mind capable of great reasoning power, and many are writers or teachers of new theories. Give them a seed and they will nurture it and make it grow. They also do well as leaders. Their thinking cannot be bound by conventional thought patterns, and they usually can and do develop their own standards, daring anyone to change their ideas. People of this decanate are not as physically restless as those with Gemini-Gemini, but they can be very nervous, an extremely restless mind wants to encompass and accumulate all possible ideas. A strong aspect to Saturn gives necessary discipline. They are more fixed and stubborn than the other Gemini decanates, and also more independent and unconventional. Often ahead of the masses in their thinking, they are capable of great things when a scientific, creative approach is combined with spirituality. By becoming more spiritually and objectively oriented, they rely less on their own reasoning and thus limit a tendency to be self-satisfied and self-centered. This decanate is similar to Mercury conjunct Uranus, which encourages intuition and original, ingenious thoughts and ideas.

Need: To use reasoning ability to objectively teach others, and to use the creative mind to help the masses.

Cancer-Cancer, The Historian: First Decanate, 0-10°, Moon-Moon, Physical

The keyword is *emotion*. These people are timid and shy in their early years, and remain somewhat introverted all their lives. There is great sympathy for others, and they are often psychic and can develop mediumship qualities. Here is the lover of the home and all domestic activities, using talents to better the home and its conditions. These people are strong parents, and remain close to home or tied to their parents throughout life. All home- and family-related activities can help to negate a tendency for moodiness. They can influence people by playing on their emotions, and therefore can control people by taking advantage of their weaknesses. Their moodiness and changeable nature comes from subconscious promptings, and security concerns can upset their emotions. They need a great deal of water in their diet, and food and a good home equate to security. They will pout when hurt, and then crawl into their shells. People with this decanate are tenacious, especially in their drive to acquire money and things. They want to know their future is safe. Even so, fears continue to be present, taking the form of self-doubt, inadequacy, and complaints. They need plenty of affection to overcome this. They are strongly affectionate themselves but because they are so easily hurt, they may appear unapproachable.

Need: To use physical energy in domesticity rather than excessive emotional outlets, and to nourish and care for all others as if they are their own.

Cancer-Scorpio, The Prophet: Second Decanate, 10-20°, Moon-Pluto, Mental

The keyword is *revelation*, and this decanate gives much fortitude, mystical talent, and mediumistic tendencies. These people have a great source of energy and are strongly sexual. When they become emotionally upset they resort to food, which is the reason many people with this placement easily gain weight. They are capable of revealing an unknown mystical truth if they develop and control their mental power, which must be balanced with their extreme sensuality. Their natures tend to be extreme and to fluctuate from deep mind power and great spiritual mysticism to sensuality. This gives the inclination to emotional outbursts of passion, jealousy, and injury. When trained in hypnosis, these people can excel in the healing profession. However, if this power is used for less than honorable purposes, it will destroy them. These people are sensitive to public needs. Much goes on beneath the surface with this decanate that others are unaware of until it suddenly surfaces, much to everyone's surprise. The Moon-Pluto influence means they are discreet and forceful.

Need: To learn to control the mind and direct its power into healing others.

Cancer-Pisces, The Musician: Third Decanate, 20-30°, Moon-Neptune, Spiritual

The keyword for this decanate is *research*. These people are capable of great spiritual research, especially in the psychic field, and this may be the most psychic of the Cancer decanates. This combination is similar to Moon conjunct Neptune and is very sympathetic and receptive to spiritual forces. These people can excel in poetry, music theory, and musical performance. Soft music can calm them when excited, and lively music can lift their mood when they are sad or depressed. Music therapy would be an excellent field for them, which is also true of the Pisces-Cancer decanate. They are the most easily influenced of all the Cancer decanates, and because they are so sensitive to sounds and unseen vibrations, they can decipher the true nature of a comment merely by hearing the tone of voice. Their curiosity can lead them to spiritual areas where only faith dwells, and they are like sponges, absorbing not only the environment but the moods of the people around them. They also can easily can tune in on the secrets of nature. At their greatest, they have deep spiritual insight. When hurt (like the other decanates of Cancer) they are can be hurt very deeply. They also have a suspicious nature and thus take few into their confidence. Some of these people become substance-abusers, and many have trouble with meditation. Hunches are often lucky.

Need: To control the emotional nature, and to study nature and reveal its secrets.

Leo-Leo, The Actor: First Decanate, 0-10°, Sun-Sun, Physical

The keyword for this decanate is *domination*. This decanate holds an abundance of ego vibrations, and thus these people tend to be dramatic and somewhat of the show-off. Proud, sincere, and vital (like the Sun that rules them), they make excellent friends and poor enemies. They have a royal air, and their love natures are powerful, intense, subjective, and attached. This love energy must be directed into appropriate channels or they will spend their time indulging in the pleasure of being in love with love. No one is more in love with the idea of love than Leo-Leo. They are self-conscious and their willpower must be directed into constructive activities or it will become destructive. They have great courage, but this courage needs to be coupled with discipline or it will dissipate. Confidence and assurance draws others to them, but this can become arrogant pride. As companions they are sought after because they are fun and exciting, and they put their all into whatever they do. Natural leaders, they also want to control and do everything in a grand manner, with a strong need to be the center of attention. Nothing is too elegant or too good for the ones they love. Faithful and loyal, they often love too much and too well, and can be hopeless romantics.

Need: To control ego and arrogance in order to become more compassionate, understanding, and loving, and to balance leadership and self-expression.

Leo-Sagittarius, The Promoter: Second Decanate, 10-20°, Sun-Jupiter, Mental

The keyword is *improvement*. These people are quick to notice weakness and have the mental power and ideas to initiate and follow through on their own progressive, improved ideas. They continually gain intellectual truth and share it with others. This position makes for freedom-loving spirits and gives philosophical leanings, along with feeding their idea of independence, which gives courage to their convictions. As a result they are apt to gain followers and become leaders. They are also the reformers and can change the world with the power of their will. This decanate also promotes optimism and integrity, and they believe luck will always favor them. They hold their heads high and walk as if they own the world. This decanate gives self-understanding in combination with an understanding of the universe, and they easily learn and grasp the laws of the universe by being aware of their own nature. They are future-oriented and want to be immortalized through their children or creative self-expression. A belief in life after death gives them more faith in themselves, what they are, and what they do. They maintain a positive outlook in their relationships and continue to love and believe in others, whether deserved or not. Taking chances with what life has to offer is second nature, and they are colorful, broad-minded people. They easily inspire and give strength to others, and can be good educators or promoters. This is a Sun-Jupiter combination, and thus generous and understanding.

Need: To give mental expression to optimistic vision so others can share hope and courage, and to promote beliefs and causes.

Leo-Aries, The Explorer: Third Decanate, 20-30°, Sun-Mars, Spiritual

The keyword is courage, and these people are also determined and have tremendous willpower that takes them far in life. They need to use these qualities for the welfare of humanity rather than for personal ego or glory. However, much of the drive for self-expression stems from a large ego rather than a desire to help humanity. They crave and usually acquire leadership positions, and the pioneering initiative of Aries pushes the Leo enthusiasm into new and different projects and adventures. They delight in anything big, bold, brave, colorful, and dramatic. Like all the Leo decanates, Leo-Aries is in love with love, and as love is their impetus, they must love their work or work with someone they love. They usually give little thought to tomorrow, and live for the moment. They put their actions behind their words, and their egos can be expressed most fully in artistic expression or with their children. They can be impatient and have a lively temper, and they are generous with self, energy, and money. It is their nature to spread warmth and laughter, and the exuberance they extend to others overflows and inspires, making them appreciated and recognized. They can be selfish (for self-glory), but they usually know themselves well, and they are decisive and do not believe in wasting time. Never content with the status quo, they explore and strive for self-expression. This is the Sun-Mars combination, so they are spontaneous and demonstrative.

Need: To explore and spiritualize the dynamic energy force for the welfare of others rather than personal glory.

Virgo-Virgo, The Analyst: First Decanate, 0-10°, Mercury-Mercury, Physical

The keyword for this decanate is *achievement*, which is accomplished through great discrimination (to decide what is important and what is not), and thoroughness. Gemini-Gemini people skim the surface and cover a lot of ground as they gather knowledge, while Virgo-Virgo people assimilate and analyze detail. These people exert energy in order to perfect or achieve the worthwhile, and should never be underestimated. They have a clarity of vision that tells them when others are lying, no matter how smooth the line, and they will never admit to being wrong. These people will not be rushed, and although they're critical of others, they do not easily accept the same. They feel they know their own faults as well as or better than anyone else and believe they are the best judges of themselves. As a result, they think they need no help from anyone. They are worriers and seem to enjoy the art of worrying, at times making it an art form. These people should concentrate on physical exercise to offset heavy mental strain. When they commit to a partnership, it is more for mental affinity than any other reason. However, do not ever underestimate the sexual prowess of a Virgo.

Need: To separate the wheat from the chaff and to put it to good use, and to accept helpful criticism from others.

Virgo-Capricorn, The Professor: Second Decanate, 10-20°, Mercury-Saturn, Mental

The keyword is *experience*, which is how these people learn. They are realistic and hardworking with a business-oriented mind, and their talents can often result in successful business ventures. This placement is good for teaching, and their minds often work like computers, assimilating information. But they need to guard against negative thinking, and use their talents in a positive, diplomatic way. This position can emphasize selfishness, so they need to be more giving. They attract an exceptional variety of experiences, both good and bad, and are obsessed with time and almost never late. Pomp and pageantry give the outlets for their tightly controlled emotions, and they have keen perceptions. They take family responsibilities seriously—love them, love their family. Saturn's influence on this decanate can stifle Mercury's thinking and action. If this happens the mind can remain closed to new ideas. Look where Saturn is by sign and house to show where stifling influences can be corrected. People with this position may lack self-confidence and spontaneity, and some of these people are inclined to be reclusive. Development may seem slow to others because of their detailed, methodical way of decision-making. This decanate also gives greater charm in later life, although they continue to have a serious outlook on life. The Mercury-Saturn influence means they are practical and precise.

Need: To use abilities and adverse conditions to push forward instead of feeling sorry for themselves and standing still in defeat.

Virgo-Taurus, The Precisionist: Third Decanate, 20-30°, Mercury-Venus, Spiritual

The keyword here is *renunciation*, which means that their greatest potential is in the area of service to others, where they do not always seek reward or notice. Look to Mercury and Venus to see the outlet for this service. These people are less self-oriented than those with the other two Virgo decanates and are more loving and less critical. They need to write or to have another creative outlet. Although this placement may deny physical children (but only if other planets concur), they seem destined to have intellectual (or spiritual) children. They can work hard, long, and devotedly without thought of any reward (although material reward will be in the back of their minds). But the ultimate reward comes in soul power for having created and brought to life some intellectual or artistic offspring. Materially they can never be paid enough for the value of their creative work, so thoroughly and devotedly is it a part of them. This placement seems to cause people to reach higher to produce long-standing products of the intellect or art objects. They love ease, comfort, and luxury and can function better when they have it. Although this placement makes them unduly sensitive to mental and affectionate vibrations, they usually are in good spirits and have a good sense of humor. They make excellent cooks and can even be gourmets. Knowing how to handle a budget is one of their finer talents unless other configurations dilute this. This Virgo is practical and concise and catches tiny errors everyone else misses. It is a decanate that indicates hereditary prestige, coming from well-situated, influential people, monetarily, intellectually, or both. This Mercury-Venus influence is diplomatic and cooperative.

Need: To be of service without notice or material reward, which can be the highest type of spiritual development.

Libra-Libra, The Artist: First Decanate, 0-10°, Venus-Venus, Physical

The keyword is *influence*. These people are romantic, gracious, diplomatic, refined, and cultured. They easily influence others and can successfully arrive at a fair policy for all concerned. Contact with others is important to them as is the need to work with others. Those with this placement attract people without effort, and they need to be with people in order to be at their best. They should channel their energy toward creativity in either the arts or decorating as beautiful surroundings are as important to them as breathing. This placement also gives a talent for social affairs and makes for the gracious host or hostess. These people are usually attractive, often with dimples. However, this decanate amplifies indecisiveness because they see both sides of a question or both points of view. Their diplomacy makes them excellent judges, with the ability to pull together both parties or issues. In their own lives they have a hard time making up their minds because they want both. They must learn to weigh the pros and cons, take a stand or make a decision, and stick to it. Even though Libra can see both sides, this does not mean they are balanced in their own lives; the purpose of Libra is to achieve this balance. They need someone to be with, someone to lean on, a partner to help make decisions. They love rich and sweet foods All of this is also true if your Sun is in the seventh house. People with this decanate also need to learn not to wear their hearts on their sleeves. If they become ill they need rest with soft music, flowers, and pleasant talk in a room with quiet colors in order to be up and around again much sooner, and at all times they need harmony.

Need: To emphasize decision-making, and to learn to love people as they find them, realizing that humans are imperfect.

Libra-Aquarius, The Debater: Second Decanate, 10-20°, Venus-Uranus, Mental

The keyword for this decanate is *equation*. The intellect is original and broad-minded, and they are controlled more by reason than emotion. This placement gives a strong mind but more fixed and not as free flowing or open as other Libra decanates. This position gives an aggressive mind, thrusting forward toward others rather than drawing inward and away. They are the leaders of more progressive movements, and many times find that the world does not embrace their personal views. So they either fail to take a personal stand or feel a compulsion to go out and fight the world in order to further their ideas. Although they are pleasant, they do not easily take orders from anyone. Enthusiastic debaters, they are logical, indecisive, kind and gentle. They rarely make an instant decision, and dislike impatient, flighty, rash or impulsive people. Their highest destiny can be reached with a soul mate. If they produce works of art, they will be out of the ordinary. This Venus-Uranus combination enhances charm and romance.

Need: People with this decanate need to unite with a soul mate and together serve humanity in the highest sense. This is the ideal toward which they must strive.

Libra-Gemini, The Reporter: Third Decanate, 20-30°, Venus-Mercury, Spiritual

The keyword for this decanate is *redemption*. These people are expressive, inquisitive, adaptable, and versatile, as well as naive and gullible. They need to restore harmony by alternating periods of activity and complete relaxation, and personal growth is linked to their level of spirituality. People with this decanate can be good reporters and journalists. Sometimes extravagant in their drive for a beautiful environment or clothing, they must be surrounded by beauty and as a result can be spendthrifts. They have brilliantly intuitive minds but can fail simply because they think they know better. This decanate indicates overall pleasant thoughts and expression, and sometimes genius as a writer or speaker. Their voices are usually pleasant, and they can talk with anyone about almost anything. Often they give the impression of doing things so easily that people think they have greater depth and talent than they do. This is the Venus-Mercury influence that indicates refinement and possibly artistic talent.

Need: To respond to the environment and people by blending their energy with their surroundings.

Scorpio-Scorpio, The Magician: First Decanate, 0-10°, Pluto-Pluto, Physical

The keyword is *rejuvenation*. Magnetic, jealous, and heroic, these people are secretive, reserved, and outwardly calm even when inwardly seething. This vital magnetism can be imparted to others, giving a natural healing ability if this power is used in a positive manner. Their physical and inner strength can be tremendous and they can withstand suffering if necessary. Whether magnificent or dangerous, they can easily fool others. eyes and you will see their inner strength. They can either selfishly love themselves or, if highly evolved, love another to the point of self-annihilation. These people often respond to questions with the frank, brutal truth, and although they often hide much, when they do speak they say it like it is. They attract either fiercely loyal, dedicated admirers or envious, spiteful enemies. They never forget. Scorpio can be cruel as well as tender, cold as well as hot. The Sun or Pluto position gives the path to follow. They can hurt others or even themselves rather than give up, and can be victims of their own power. Their strength is dauntless.

Need: To use their great strength and power to heal others with the energy that flows from them.

Scorpio-Pisces, The Researcher: Second Decanate, 10-20o, Pluto-Neptune, Mental

The keyword for this decanate is *sacrifice*. At their best these people are committed in their service to humanity. Saints or devils, they are either spiritual or bent upon destroying themselves and others to make a point, so their power needs to be channeled. Scorpio reconstructs, rejuvenates, or causes death. People with this decanate especially need to watch their alcohol intake. They also have great mental power for research and can get to the bottom of anything. When this ability is used to best advantage, they seek the secrets of life, and when subconscious ideas are brought forth and given to the world, they become powerful vehicles for good. At worst they can become alcoholic, neurotic, and drug-dependent, feeling like helpless martyrs mired in useless self-pity. Psychic impressions take the form of fearful apprehension or constructive inspiration. They never forget, nor will they give up until the enemy is destroyed or they have accomplished a constructive goal. Their all-encompassing drives can cause emotional illness or give them mental strength above and beyond the average. This Neptune-Pluto influence gives the ability to transcend self in order to help the masses.

Need: To use their innate talents and research ability to find and promote mental healing so people can live more fully.

Scorpio-Cancer, The Detective: Third Decanate, 20-30°, Pluto-Moon, Spiritual

The keyword here is *acquisition*. These people are tenacious and home loving, and once they get something, it is forever. This position gives great psychic power and must be used for good or it is absorbed into the system, where it can destroy. They need people of the opposite sex to stimulate their ambitions and ideals because they need an emotional outlet. People with this decanate can be chivalrous, stern on the outside and soft on the inside, which also endows great sexual potency. They have a particular way of speaking and their friendly manners can be misleading; only direct eye contact can reveal their true feelings. Inside they are tough and determined, and they have explosive tempers. This influence also causes an insatiable drive to possess the material objects of life. They are just as relentless in their pursuit of a romantic interest. A Moon-Pluto combination indicates that they are secretive and seclusive.

Need: To learn that spirituality is the only real possession and that all the material success in this world will not provide peace.

Sagittarius-Sagittarius, The Evangelist: First Decanate, 0-10°, Jupiter-Jupiter, Physical

The keyword is *zeal*. This position gives a witty and jovial nature, and these people are the talkers, the travelers, and the optimists. They are restless and easily bored, and have a kinship with nature (physical nature) and all living creatures. When highly developed, they feel an enduring connection with the universe and place trust in its direction. They can be gossipy and sociable, and excel in sales. There is a constant alertness for new facts, and they are sure they have a definite mission in life—to teach others the true cosmic facts. At times shockingly direct in speech, they are unaware of this because the motive is pure honesty. All Sagittarius decanates indicate bright, alert eyes, and people with this decanate move fast and find it difficult to stand or sit still. They fear almost nothing, and risk excites them. People influenced by this decanate dream big dreams and aim high. They love to travel and spread the word whether they are ministers or evangelists. These people take chances on anything and love to gamble, although not necessarily with money. They simply have to put something at risk.

Need: To use their zeal to minister to and teach others the universal truths and to travel far and wide.

Sagittarius-Aries, The Philosopher: Second Decanate, 10-20°, Jupiter-Mars, Mental

The keyword for this decanate is *exploration*. These people can be foolhardy but also generous, prophetic, adventurous, and independent. They are sometimes pioneers in teaching, and can be outstanding leaders and executives. The mind is ever alert to higher vibrations, and people with this decanate disregard established mental values in favor of individual, creative thought. The element of risk excites them, they love anything that goes fast, and resist confinement. All decanates of this approach love with speed, but unlike the first two decanates, which have difficulty with commitment, this one is more open to permanence. Even so, they seek casual relationships that fit better with their independent, adventuresome natures, and are not interested in permanent ties that limit them. Strong intellectual powers can be muted by sarcasm or a lack of ability to keep secrets. They can remember abstract truths but forget ordinary little details of daily living, as in the true absent-minded professor. This Mars-Jupiter influence signifies people who are eager, enthusiastic, and lively.

Need: To explore new fields of knowledge and then disseminate the information through publishing or teaching.

Sagittarius-Leo, The Ambassador: Third Decanate, 20-30°, Jupiter-Sun, Spiritual

The keyword is *enlightenment*. These people are romantic and idealistic, combining ego with the power of the superconscious mind. A noble decanate, they have the ability to perceive things as they are and to impart this to others in a spiritual way. These people can reach higher states of con through and by personal enlightenment that is spiritually illuminating. People with this decanate love applause for they are happiest when performing, whether on stage or while socializing, and they never seem to grow old. Although happy and exuberant, their tempers can flare when anyone tries to force them. They will never turn away from a problem or ask for any help from others as they fight their own battles and solve their own problems. At times they can be overly confident. This Sagittarius-Leo influence seeks a love relationship that is also an adventure, and Sun-Jupiter enhances optimism and intuition.

Need: To resist excessive pursuit of pleasure and become an example of nobility, and to teach the art of true caring and spiritual love.

Capricorn-Capricorn, The Executive: First Decanate, 0-10°, Saturn-Saturn, Physical

The keyword is *organization*. These people can be unimaginative but practical, thrifty, ambitious, and persistent in attaining goals. They, more than others, realize the value of system and organization in getting things done, and their greatest talent is merging opposing forces. People with this decanate can be very serious with an invisible melancholy, and need to stop and look at the lighter side of life. They can be social climbers. They seldom fail for they let others first test the way as they learn by observation. Then they come along and do a fantastic job, polishing, and organizing. They always look ahead, prepared for opportunity when it comes and before anyone else even knows it has arrived. All Capricorns use people to make their way, but as they see it, people are meant to help each other. They put up with a lot, but when they have had it, they have had it. Like the other two Capricorn decanates, they do not rush into marriage because for them it must last. So they consider all the angles before tying the bonds.

Need: To organize physical forces and people in order to manifest the greatest good for the greatest number of people, and to execute better conditions for humankind.

Capricorn-Taurus, The Architect: Second Decanate, 10-20°, Saturn-Venus, Mental

The keyword for this decanate is *dedication*. These people are extremely loyal and have great endurance, and can have musical or artistic talent. They can make the most of their environment, utilizing all conditions for their purposes When they encounter setbacks, their great endurance allows them to carry on. They need to build something of value that transcends their lifetime, and have no patience with unsound methods or those that are not based in common sense. These people seem harmless and can be very gentle, kind and helpful, but they are rugged. They are aware of getting the greatest value from everything, either organizing methods for their own good (unevolved), or for the greater good of all people (evolved). When they love others, they are capable of deep suffering and stand by them in the face of all trouble and danger. The Venus-Saturn influence with this decanate means they are faithful and loyal above and beyond the ordinary.

Need: To organize a method by which they can dedicate themselves to accomplishment, and to build an ever-lasting monument.

Capricorn-Virgo, The Idealist: Third Decanate, 20-30°, Saturn-Mercury, Spiritual

The keyword is *idealism*. This decanate is more discriminating than the others, and increases the intellectual faculties. These people are capable of viewing the spiritual ideal and then expressing it in a concrete form. Their imagination is greater than the other decanates and, when united with their faculty for intense labor, brings them ultimate success. They are untiring workers. These people are best when following their own ideas. When other people play, they never sway from the path, continuing to work steadily toward their goals with faith in the security of a disciplined endeavor. They make excellent mathematicians, researchers, and trouble-shooters. Their highest spiritual inspiration can be expressed in building something concrete, and they put much thought into anything before taking action. Everything needs a spiritual purpose behind it, and there is in turn a purpose in everything they do. The road ahead is always in mind, and nothing blocks their view of goals and the future. They may have a talent for technical writing or be involved in developing theories that can serve others in the future, leading to a better and richer life. This Mercury-Saturn combination indicates an exacting and shrewd mind.

Need: To build something concrete that has its roots in inspiration or an ideal, and to relate both what is important and unimportant in life.

Aquarius-Aquarius, The Scientist: First Decanate, 0-10°, Uranus-Uranus, Physical

The keyword is *originality*. These people are unconventional and broad-minded, and this position gives intimate knowledge of human nature. They know how to handle people and are progressive in their attitudes. This decanate indicates inventiveness and thus is good for the scientific field. They have their own ideas and are keenly interested in education, and their true mission is to share their enthusiasm about advanced ideas with others, believing as they do in the ultimate potential of every human being. Yet they are also realistic. They are also people of the unexpected, and can cut others short with a surprising or shocking statement, while giving the impression of being a million miles away and leaving others feeling as though they are missing something somewhere. These people are natural rebels who think old ways are outdated and that innovative thinking is what society needs. They have few friends, but many acquaintances, seeking quantity rather than quality, and finding it difficult to maintain a steady relationship for more than a limited period. In the middle of a crowd they seem alone and isolated even though they are friendly, sociable, and unpredictable. Yet they can stick to a cause beyond all understanding of others. They tend to live in the future and feel disoriented when the present demand attention.

Need: To impart their innovative ideas to others.

Aquarius-Gemini, The Aviator: Second Decanate, 10-20°, Uranus-Mercury, Mental

The keyword is *inspiration*. These people can be eager, nervous and excitable, with a mind that travels the universe while still at home. They are exceptionally curious, but their ideas should be used for humanity and not just for their own thoughts. They have a never-ending source of fascinating material, and thus make good writers because of their ability to acquire information and knowledge from seemingly invisible sources and then present it to others in a most interesting and convincing way. Their inspiration comes from others, and they constantly ask questions, often with little tact, and are compulsively curious about people's deepest and most intimate feelings. When answers are provided, they become bored and, without notice, turn their interest elsewhere. They also can give the impression that they're not actually listening. This of course can upset people. They refuse to conform and need to show this nonconformity in an obvious way. There can be dual sexuality if other factors indicate the same, and like most Aquarians, they aren't as highly sexed as other signs unless their charts show a strong, sexual Mars and other physically-oriented aspects. This Mercury-Uranus influence is very intellectually creative.

Need: To inspire others with the vastness of material at their disposal.

Aquarius-Libra, The Humanitarian: Third Decanate, 20-30°, Uranus-Venus, Spiritual

The keyword is *association*. This is the diplomat. Their greatest work can be done in partnership with someone of the opposite sex. In a romantic partnership they need true love and spiritual love. Love is a reforming agent in their lives, and without it they disconnect from the cosmic source that inspires and directs them, stifling their life work. When they follow their heart and find companionship in the highest sense, they are half of an effective team working for others. They either accept true love or repress and stop growing. These people lower their heads when thinking or after having been asked a question. Like all decanates, this one can indicate genius or eccentricity, depending upon aspects in the chart. They can be highly nervous, and can tune their senses to higher spheres of thought waves; with favorable aspects, this can indicate a talent for prophecy. All decanates of Uranus are an odd and curious mixture of eccentric instability, and instinctive. This Venus-Uranus influence is associated with people who are enchanting and unconventional in their attitude on love and marriage.

Need: To combine knowledge with a mate and use it to better humanity.

Pisces-Pisces, The Poet: First Decanate, 0-10°, Neptune-Neptune, Physical

The keyword is *perception*. Here, the self has to be sacrificed in some way in order to fulfill the promise of this decanate. These people are seers who can easily comprehend the esoteric through astrology or another vehicle. They, like Scorpio and Cancer, are detectives and are good this kind of work. It is not easy for them to struggle or fight their way upstream as they would rather go with the current. However, they must meet the challenge for it is the only way they will find true peace and contentment. Taking the easy way is a trap for Pisces-Pisces. Very little in life can arouse them to forceful action. They see the world through rose-colored glasses as the real world seems too harsh for their poetic nature to behold, and they are very sensitive to conditions around them. The choice is theirs to advance to greater growth toward their spiritual destiny in self-service or to resist the struggle and hold back in self-pity. Because they do not easily envision the future, they can only take it on blind faith and commit without a guarantee. They can go to the heights of a dedicated professional life with great spiritual love or to the depths of false emotion.

Need: To use their talents and psychic expression for others to benefit from and enjoy.

Pisces-Cancer, The Dreamer: Second Decanate, 10-20°, Neptune-Moon, Mental

The keyword is *sympathy*. These people are easily hurt and apt to withdraw when this occurs. They are timid and strongly sympathetic to others but need to learn to control their moodiness. Worry can cause ulcers. They grasp the concept of universal brotherhood and know their spiritual mission in life. However, they must learn not to worry but to cultivate peace-of-mind. When mental sufferings are alleviated they can help their fellow man with whom they so easily sympathize. This mental decanate can give esoteric wisdom to a greater or lesser degree, depending upon how much they control their negative moods. They should avoid alcohol and drugs, and need the freedom to dream and experience strong feelings and sensations. Their aptitude for prophecy depends entirely upon whether they embrace selfless service or self-pity. Some excel in the entertainment world. They never forget a hurt, and loss of hope can threaten their security. They may laugh to control their tears or to hide their feelings. This is a Moon-Neptune influence, which means they are impressionable and perceptive.

Need: To use the talent of sympathy and compassion to ease the burdens of others.

Pisces-Scorpio, The Mystic: Third Decanate, 20-30°, Neptune-Pluto, Spiritual

The keyword is *denial*. These people can be penetrating and magnetic, and have a deeply sensuous nature. Their spiritual mission is to prepare people for life after death, and their research (at which they excel) should be in that area. This gives eventful lives and the ability to succeed in a wide variety of careers. They are capable of reaching high development in psychic research and then teaching others about the unseen world and how to follow a life that will help prepare them for life after death. Very little will provoke these people to violent action, but they do have a mean temper when pushed too far. They can be sarcastic and cutting if necessary. Because of the belief that they will live forever, they do not always take care of themselves as they should. However, they also have the power to heal themselves. They can hypnotize themselves into or out of anything they choose. This decanate imprisons some in their sexual nature to the exclusion of other parts of a relationship. Turned to a higher level, their nature can be one of sainthood and extreme self-denial. These people are little understood and few, if any, know them as they do not reveal themselves. They are on a ray that others cannot easily tune into, and for this reason they are often lonely. Their best expression from one level of understanding to another is through music, which can carry them forth to communication with another that goes beyond words. Their extreme beauty is little seen, let alone understood. This combination of Neptune-Pluto means they are regenerative, capable of tearing something out by the roots and starting over again.

Need: To learn to use their magnetic and penetrating nature to communicate the magic of love that goes beyond words, and to live and speak from the spiritual plane.

Interpreting the Decanates for Other Planets

Although the preceding interpretations are oriented to the Sun signs, they can be read for the other planets: Sun (ego); Moon (emotional nature, women, mother, home); Mercury (environment, brothers and sisters, mental pursuits, conscious mind and expression); Venus (love nature, ideal woman for a man); Mars (passions, energy, ideal man for a woman); Jupiter (religious and philosophical nature, higher mind, long travels, method of expansion); Saturn (discipline, restrictive nature); Neptune (inspiration, higher spiritual nature, illusion); Uranus (the enlightener, the awakener, creative thinking, the place where one is unconventional and erratic); Pluto (regeneration and rejuvenation, sex, corporate money); North Node (place of new growth;

South Node (place of knowledge already gained and known, karmic). Especially consider interpretations to the Sun, Moon, and Ascendant, for it is these three areas that determine the initial picture of the individual, past, present, and future. The Moon is the past, the Sun is the present, and the Ascendant is the future.

The decanate of the Sun describes the ego or the means whereby you shine and why you fail to shine, according to the aspects involved. The decanate of the Moon shows the nature of the emotional make-up, how feelings originate, or why they operate. In a man's chart, the Moon in a particular decanate shows his attitude toward women or the type of woman he attracts. The decanate description could then be a description of a woman, or women in his life, including his mother.

Chapter 3

Decanate Aspects and Synastry

Conventional aspects such as trines, sextiles, conjunctions, oppositions, and squares should always be used and never disregarded. But a secondary, more esoteric, consideration should be included: decanate aspects, which are important not only in individual chart interpretation but in comparison between charts. A decanate aspect between two charts can be very binding (especially if Saturn is involved, for it seems to indicate other life connections or soul-linkage. The sign ruler is always the projector, whereas the decanate ruler is the receiver. Note also that the difference between the sign ruler and decanate ruler: the ruler of the sign has an outer nature, and the decanate ruler has an inner nature.

The following will serve as guidance for further interpretation when the signs match even though they do not make a conventional aspect.

Comparative Decanates

Aries-Aries (first decanate, 0-10°): The first decanate is oriented to the physical influence and the sign's interpretation. It stands alone because it does not have a decanate aspect.

Aries-Leo (second decanate, 10-20°, mental) and Leo-Aries (third decanate, 20-30°, spiritual): Also check for a conventional Mars-Sun aspect between charts or in an individual chart for an esoteric or spiritual connection.

Aries-Sagittarius (third decanate, 20-30°, spiritual) and Sagittarius-Aries (second decanate, 10-20°, mental): Check Jupiter-Mars between charts for conventional aspect.

Taurus-Taurus (first decanate, 10-20°): The first decanate is oriented to the physical influence and the sign's interpretation. It stands alone because it does not have a decanate aspect.

Taurus-Virgo (second decanate, l0-20°, mental) and Virgo-Taurus (third decanate, 20-30°, spiritual): Check Mercury-Venus in the charts for a conventional aspect.

Taurus-Capricorn (third decanate, 20-30°, spiritual) and Capricorn-Taurus (second decanate, 10-20°, mental): Check for a Saturn-Venus conventional aspect.

Gemini-Gemini (first decanate, 0-10°): The first decanate is oriented to the physical influence and the sign's interpretation. It stands alone because it does not have a decanate aspect.

Gemini-Libra (second decanate, 10-20°, mental) and Libra-Gemini (third decanate, 20-30°, spiritual): Check for Venus-Mercury conventional aspect.

Gemini-Aquarius (third decanate, 20-30°, spiritual) and Aquarius-Gemini (second decanate, 10-20°, mental): Check for a Uranus-Mercury conventional aspect.

Cancer-Cancer (first decanate, 0-10°): The first decanate is oriented to the physical influence and the sign's interpretation. It stands alone because it does not have a decanate aspect.

Cancer-Scorpio (second decanate, 10-20°, mental) and Scorpio-Cancer (third decanate, 20-30°, spiritual): Check Moon-Pluto for conventional aspect.

Cancer-Pisces (third decanate, 20-30°, spiritual) and Pisces-Cancer (second decanate, 10-20°, mental): Check for a Neptune-Moon conventional aspect.

Leo-Leo (first decanate, 0-10°): The first decanate is oriented to the physical influence and the sign's interpretation. It stands alone because it does not have a decanate aspect.

Leo-Sagittarius (second decanate, 10-20°, mental) and Sagittarius-Leo (third decanate, 20-30°, spiritual): Check for a Sun-Jupiter conventional aspect.

Leo-Aries (third decanate, 20-30°, spiritual) and Aries-Leo (second decanate, 10-20°, mental): Check for a Mars-Sun conventional aspect.

Virgo-Virgo (first decanate, 0-10°): The first decanate is oriented to the physical influence and the sign's interpretation. It stands alone because it does not have a decanate aspect.

Virgo-Capricorn (second decanate, 10-20°, mental) and Capricorn-Virgo (third decanate, 20-30°, spiritual): Check Mercury-Saturn for a conventional aspect.

Virgo-Taurus (third decanate, 20-30°, spiritual) and Taurus-Virgo (second decanate, 10-20°, mental): Check Mercury-Venus for a conventional aspect.

Libra-Libra (first decanate, 0-10°): The first decanate is oriented to the physical influence and the sign's interpretation. It stands alone because it does not have a decanate aspect.

Libra-Aquarius (second decanate, 10-20°, mental) and Aquarius-Libra (third decanate, 20-30°, spiritual): Check Venus-Uranus for a conventional aspect.

Libra-Gemini (third decanate, 20-30°, spiritual) and Gemini-Libra (second decanate, 10-20°, mental): Check Mercury-Venus for a conventional aspect.

Scorpio-Scorpio (first decanate, 0-10°): The first decanate is oriented to the physical influence and the sign's interpretation. It stands alone because it does not have a decanate aspect.

Scorpio-Pisces (second decanate, 10-20°, mental) and Pisces-Scorpio (third decanate, 20-30°, spiritual): Check for a Neptune-Pluto aspect. This may be a generation or group tie from the past or a soul relationship where more than one person is involved.

Scorpio-Cancer (third decanate, 20-30°, spiritual) and Cancer-Scorpio (second decanate, 10-20°, mental): Check Moon-Pluto for a conventional aspect.

Sagittarius-Sagittarius (first decanate, 0-10°): The first decanate is oriented to the physical influence and the sign's interpretation. It stands alone because it does not have a decanate aspect.

Sagittarius-Aries (second decanate, 10-20°, mental) and Aries-Sagittarius (third decanate, 20-30°, spiritual): Check Mars-Jupiter for a conventional aspect.

Sagittarius-Leo (third decanate, 20-30°, spiritual) and Leo-Sagittarius (second decanate, 10-20°, mental): Check Sun-Jupiter for a conventional aspect.

Capricorn-Capricorn (first decanate, 0-10°): The first decanate is oriented to the physical influence and the sign's interpretation. It stands alone because it does not have a decanate aspect.

Capricorn-Taurus (second decanate, 10-20°, mental) and Taurus-Capricorn (third decanate, 20-30°, spiritual): Check Venus-Saturn for a conventional aspect.

Capricorn-Virgo (third decanate, 20-30°, spiritual) and Virgo-Capricorn (second decanate, 10-20°, mental): Check Mercury-Saturn for a conventional aspect.

Aquarius-Aquarius (first decanate, 0-10°): The first decanate is oriented to the physical influence and the sign's interpretation. It stands alone because it does not have a decanate aspect.

Aquarius-Gemini (second decanate, 10-20°, mental) and Gemini-Aquarius (third decanate, 20-30°, spiritual): Check Uranus-Mercury for a conventional aspect.

Aquarius-Libra (third decanate, 20-30°, spiritual) and Libra-Aquarius (second decanate, 10-20°, mental): Check Venus-Uranus for a conventional aspect.

Pisces-Pisces (first decanate, 0-10°): The first decanate is oriented to the physical influence and the sign's interpretation. It stands alone because it does not have a decanate aspect.

Pisces-Cancer (second decanate, 10-20°, mental) and Cancer-Pisces (third decanate, 20-30°, spiritual): Check Moon-Neptune for a conventional aspect.

Pisces-Scorpio (third decanate, 10-20°, spiritual) and Scorpio-Pisces (second decanate, 10-20°, mental): Check Pluto-Neptune for a conventional aspect. This is a group or generational tie.

The synastry patterns presented above are theories I developed after extensive research, and they have worked consistently for me. Conventional aspect considerations in synastry show the *now*. The decanate aspects show past connections or the soul's ability to recognize and to blend the past with the present. Sometimes the decanate sign co-ruler, such as Gemini-Aquarius, third decanate, will compare with the physical, first decanate, Aquarius. The decanate sign (Aquarius in this case) is projected onto a physical manifestation through association with the first decanate in individual charts and in synastry. It then takes on a physical experience. Some examples follow:

Aries Leo to first decanate Leo

Taurus-Virgo to first decanate Virgo

Gemini-Libra to first decanate Libra

Cancer-Scorpio to first decanate Scorpio

Leo-Sagittarius to first decanate Sagittarius

Virgo-Capricorn to first decanate Capricorn

Libra-Aquarius to first decanate Aquarius

Scorpio-Pisces to first decanate Pisces

Sagittarius-Aries to first decanate Aries

Capricorn-Taurus to first decanate Taurus

Aquarius-Gemini to first decanate Gemini

Pisces-Cancer to first decanate Cancer

Aries-Sagittarius to first decanate Sagittarius

Taurus-Capricorn to first decanate Capricorn

Gemini-Aquarius to first decanate Aquarius

Cancer-Pisces to first decanate Pisces

Leo-Aries to first decanate Aries

Virgo-Taurus to first decanate Taurus

Libra-Gemini to first decanate Gemini

Scorpio-Cancer to first decanate Cancer

Sagittarius-Leo to first decanate Leo

Capricorn-Virgo to first decanate Virgo

Aquarius-Libra to first decanate Libra

Pisces-Scorpio to first decanate Scorpio

This influence seems to operate when the decanate co-ruler is not turned outward through the sign and house affairs or when there is a weakness and/or debility.

Esoteric Patterns

This same decanate method of aspecting can be used in individual charts. First, find the decanate aspect, such as Neptune in Libra (Aquarius) to Venus in Aquarius (Libra). This appears to be something unfinished from the past (life). Now look for a conventional aspect of Venus to Uranus, which in this case is Uranus in a man's seventh house and Venus in Aquarius in the third house. Marriage, love, a brother or sister, communication, and much traveling are involved in the new learning experiences. This man will also experience enlightenment (or break free) as a result of a woman, and the promise of this aspect will not be fulfilled in this lifetime until this happens.

Somehow the past sacrifice related to Neptune will have to be resolved, or repaid, first. Uranus will prevail and there will be an unusual marriage to an above-average woman who is unconventional and/or perhaps creative and intellectual. With Venus trine Uranus in his chart, (the aspect pertinent to this life), she (the woman in his life) will not be eccentric, which would be true if this Venus-Uranus aspect were a square.

Example Comparisons Between Charts

A man's Sun in Gemini (Libra decanate) compared with a woman's Venus in Libra (Gemini decanate): This satisfies the man's ego, and he can truly be himself with this woman who knows how to love him.

A man's Mars Sagittarius (Leo) decanate compared with a woman's Moon in Leo (Sagittarius decanate): There is an emotional and physical attraction and a rare kind of magnetism. His physical drive and passion will blend with the emotional expression of the woman.

The Moon in Aries (Sagittarius decanate) compared with the Ascendant in Sagittarius (Aries decanate): one person's emotional nature understands and blends well with the outgoing personality (Ascendant) of the other.

Venus in Gemini (Aquarius decanate) compared with Venus in Aquarius (Gemini decanate): This is true of any Venus comparison with any sign. Another example would be Venus in Leo (Sagittarius decanate) with Venus in Sagittarius (Leo decanate). This means they may love each other, but their love is more like looking in the mirror. However, this is better when a woman has Venus in Gemini (Aquarius decanate) compared with a man's Sun or Mars in Aquarius (Gemini decanate). It would also be positive if the Venus in Gemini (Aquarius decanate) compares with a man's Sun in Aquarius (first decanate) or Sun in Gemini (first decanate). If her Venus in Gemini (Aquarius decanate) compares with the Sun in Aquarius (first decanate) or the Sun in Gemini in a man's chart, there would be a strong physical reaction between them and/or a lot of physical activity involved in their relationship because the man's Sun is in the physical decanate and physical activity would satisfy his ego. Her Venus, in the spiritual decanate, would make the relationship between them physical-spiritual. In the final analysis, the physical experiences would (or should) have a spiritual meaning for them.

These aspects between decanates, which are mental and spiritual influences, respond to a higher soul union developed from many past lives, past soul origins, or development. In any case, it is a karmic or higher-level consciousness bond. In chart comparisons the decanate aspects can influence all the planets and the Nodes. The Ascendant may be considered but does not always respond to the influence except when in relationship to the first decanate of another planet, Mars, or between the rulers of the decanate signs being considered. For example, if decanate aspects are found, there seems to be soul connection from the past. In any event there is a strong mental and spiritual bond in this life that is further defined by the nature of the planet involved and the house placement.

More Examples of Decanate Synastry

Moon in 29 Aries (third decanate, Sagittarius) compared with Jupiter in 18 Sagittarius (second decanate, Aries): Look to the nature of the Moon and Jupiter planets to see what kind of mental and spiritual connection exists in this life, and to the house positions to see how it comes about. To find an intimate and intense soul relationship from the past, check to see if there is a conventional aspect between rulers of the signs involved in the decanate aspect.

The above comparison would involve Mars (ruler of Aries) and Jupiter (ruler of Sagittarius). If there is a conventional aspect between Mars and Jupiter in the charts, a more intimate connection from a past life is indicated as well as a further experience in this life. To determine what was involved in the past life, interpret Jupiter (religion, philosophy, faraway travels, etc.) and Mars (passion, war, leadership, pioneer). It could be interpreted as someone traveling far away to war, a religious crusade, or coming to America from a foreign land and pioneering the West (or all three). It can also show that a marriage was involved.

Naturally the house placements of these planets must be taken into consideration but only the house placements of Mars and Jupiter show conditions from the past life that have a compulsive effect in this life. The original decanate aspect (Moon-Jupiter) and its house placements show how it comes about this time. In this existence Jupiter has a strong influence again, but this time it could mean anything from higher education, much travel, or both. In other words, Jupiter overlaps from one life to another. Perhaps the vibration of Jupiter between them could be satisfied by disseminating knowledge or religion, or some kind of moral commitment between them. In this example, do not overlook aspects to the ninth and fourth house cusps in order to show a clearer nature of what must be accomplished in depicting the full picture.

If Venus is involved in this kind of decanate aspect between two people, it shows a love relationship that started in a past life and is to be continued or completed in this life. Another planet placed in a Venus-ruled house would further explain the conditions about the past life *if aspected to the rulers of the original decanate sign aspect* or a contributing influence of the present life if aspected to the decanate aspect itself. Naturally this would be the Libra house (seventh, marriage) or the Taurus house (second, resources), or if Venus aspects the cusp of the fifth house.

Again, both decanate aspect and the conventional rulership aspect are needed to show strong past life linkage. I cannot over-emphasize this.

For example, Venus in Gemini (Aquarius decanate; rulers Mercury and Uranus) compared with Venus in Aquarius (Gemini decanate). Venus in one chart is in the eighth house and Venus in the other chart is in the second. This indicates additional conditions from a past life. There is a conventional aspect between the chart rulers. Mercury is conjunct Uranus in Gemini in the seventh house, which shows the new experience for the person in whose seventh house the conjunction occurs. In the other chart, this conjunction is in the eighth house, and it is the eighth house experience that has to be completed and fulfilled in this life. Remember, it is love between two people that is under consideration—past, present, and future.

For the Venus in Gemini person, because Mercury is also conjunct Venus in Gemini, this indicates a problem with communication in a past life as well as a condition related to her partner's money and sex.

The past is described by the decanate signs, planets aspected, and house positions (sometimes a subconscious compulsion in this life). The identification and destiny of the present and future are described by the conventional aspects, signs and house positions.

One young man has Saturn in Sagittarius (Leo decanate) compared with Neptune in Leo (Sagittarius decanate). The rulers are Sun and Jupiter, which shows a family or legal relationship. There is no conventional aspect with the Sun and Jupiter between charts, so there is no karmic experience in this life even though they will recognize each other and feel a connection.

A young woman has Mars in Leo (Sagittarius decanate) compared with an older woman whose Mars is in Sagittarius (Leo decanate). There is an exact forty-degree nonagen aspect of the young woman's Sun to the older woman's Jupiter, and the older woman's Sun is square the younger woman's Jupiter. The position by house of Mars and Jupiter shows how this will play out in this life: the rulership aspects show that the older woman will teach the younger woman. The double aspect shows the two lives they apparently experienced together. I interpret them in one life as very close friends and in another life as sisters.

Another set of charts seems to be verified by the conduct of two people in this life: They have a Mars conjunct Jupiter decanate aspect in their charts. The interpretation of the rulers of the signs involved shows that they may have been married in a past life. There is no regular conventional aspect between these rulers so it appears it will not lead to marriage in this life. If there had been a conventional aspect to the rulers of the signs involved in the Mars-Jupiter conjunction, it would lead to a marriage or union in this life. They may have a physical marriage and live together for awhile, but it may not lead to a legal or public union.

Another example: South Node in Leo (Sagittarius decanate) to Mars in Sagittarius (Leo decanate). The rulers are Sun and Jupiter. There exists between these two much happiness and real understanding. The Sun of one person is trine Jupiter in the other chart, which could indicate a spiritual marriage or legal union.

In another chart, Mars in Sagittarius (Aries decanate) is compared with another's Moon in Aries (Sagittarius decanate). The Moon and Mars and house position show how it will come about in this life. The fact that there is a decanate aspect shows a past life experience, but it takes a conventional aspect to the rulers to indicate a more intimate involvement. Rulers Mars and Jupiter describe conditions of the relationship in the past which could have been marriage. If there is a conventional aspect between Mars and Jupiter this couple will continue a relationship in this life and will be married again. House position is also important. The kind of aspect is important, for if the conventional aspect is a square or an opposition there could be danger of a separation or interference by a third party before any permanent arrangement is agreed upon. The interference in this case does not have to be a person; it can be a project and/or a vocation that takes priority with one of the parties.

If there is more than one decanate aspect between charts, it can show more than one life together, with each decanate aspect showing and describing that life.

A South Node in Leo (Sagittarius decanate) with Mars in Sagittarius (Leo decanate) and rulers Sun and Jupiter could indicate one was a parent to the other. This Sun is square Jupiter by conventional aspect, and Jupiter is in the eleventh house, which indicates they were friends once and there was an intellectual difference or conflict that caused separation. This time they must solve this difference.

Individual Charts

A man has the Sun in Capricorn (Virgo decanate) and Mars in the first decanate of Virgo. Physical energy and action can be transferred or redirected through his Mars in Virgo in the ninth house (energy in study, travel, and religion) in the form of always looking for greener pastures to satisfy his ego. This is especially true if he is not satisfied with his income because his Sun is in the second house.

Another example in an individual chart is Neptune in Libra (Aquarius decanate). This person's Mercury is in the first decanate of Aquarius in the second house, and Neptune is in the tenth house. He would want an ideal profession or always be more or less dissatisfied with the existing one. When dissatisfied he would express this by trying to make more money, becoming involved in gathering more resources of all kinds, much travel, or great concern with and for his siblings.

A woman has Uranus in Gemini (Aquarius decanate) in the seventh house and Mercury in the first decanate of Aquarius in the third house. When she cannot express the way she feels within a deep relationship or with her marriage, she redirects it for short little trips around town with her sisters or to pursue intellectual interest.

Extra Considerations

A person who has many planets in the first decanate will concentrate on the physical plane in this life. He or she will experience much action and use a lot of energy in the pursuit of his or her destiny.

Sometimes you will notice a family or group with a similar set of decanate aspects between them (similar rulerships of these decanate aspects) relating them one to the other and to all in the group. This can mean they were closely associated as a group in past lives.

A person having many planets in the second decanate will concentrate on the mental interpretations of life in the drive to meet his or her destiny.

The person who has more planets in third decanates will have a spiritual destiny and needs to see life in a more spiritual light. If he or she tries to pursue life with only a physical consideration, success will not be achieved.

When looking for the greatest number of decanate placements, include the Ascendant, Midheaven, Nodes, and Part of Fortune.

Subjective Rulership of Decanates

Most of us have a subjective outlook on life, so take note of the following Sepharial rulerships of the decanates to see where your weakness may lie. It may be a place where you need greater cosmic awareness.

The order of rotation of planetary rulerships of the decanates is Mars, Sun, Venus, Mercury, Moon, Saturn, Jupiter. This is repeated over and over.

Decanate	Ruler	Subjective Influence
Aries, First	Mars	Innovative, passionate, excessive fearlessness
Aries, Second	Sun	Ego, pride oriented
Aries, Third	Venus	Love, beauty, and original artistic talent

Taurus, First	Mercury	Conscious awareness of surroundings, mental
Taurus, Second	Moon	Emotional and feeling oriented, domestic
Taurus, Third	Saturn	Serious, disciplined, and overly dutiful
Gemini, First	Jupiter	Optimistic, understanding, overly eager
Gemini, Second	Mars	Use of energy scattering hither and yon
Gemini, Third	Sun	Individualistic, seeking enjoyment
Cancer, First	Venus	Love, excessive gathering of things
Cancer, Second	Mercury	Brothers, sisters, environmental sensitivity
Cancer, Third	Moon	Feelings, home, changeable, easily hurt
Leo, First	Saturn	Overly disciplined and dutiful to lovers
Leo, Second	Jupiter	Gambler, religious, exaggerating
Leo, Third	Mars	Passionate, adventurous
Virgo, First	Sun	Ego satisfied by analyzing and criticizing
Virgo, Second	Venus	Perfection for love and beauty
Virgo, Third	Mercury	Conscious mind oriented to literary
Libra, First	Moon	Feelings for mate, or sensitivity to art
Scorpio, First	Mars	Energy, passions, sexual pride, destructive
Scorpio, Second	Sun	Domination of others, glory seeking
Scorpio, Third	Venus	Possessive love and secretive associations
Sagittarius, First	Mercury	Very conscious understanding, talkative
Sagittarius, Second	Moon	Feeling excessively fortunate, or detached
Sagittarius, Third	Saturn	Disciplined scientific talent, or religious
Capricorn, First	Jupiter	Integrity with ambition, starts big
Capricorn, Second	Mars	Much ambitious action, desires to be first
Capricorn, Third	Sun	Ambition for glory and status
Aquarius, First	Venus	Congenial with friends, beauty conscious
Aquarius, Second	Mercury	Creative mind, independent, nervous
Aquarius, Third	Moon	Erratic emotionalism, feelings for friends
Pisces, First	Saturn	Excessive sacrifice for duty, depressive
Pisces, Second	Jupiter	Spiritual, intellectually sensitive
Pisces, Third	Mars	Secretly aggressive, sensitive passions

Try these subjective influences in comparison between charts or aspects in your own chart, and expand them with your own imagination and insight. Compare the second decanate of Aries with the third decanate of Gemini, the first decanate of Virgo, the second decanate of Scorpio, or the third decanate of Capricorn. All are ruled by the Sun and can show a relationship not indicated elsewhere.

The third decanate of Aries seems to identify with the first decanate of Cancer, the second decanate of Virgo, the third decanate of Scorpio, and the first decanate of Aquarius.

The rulerships stated above have an inner, or subjective, significance. The conventional or objective influences seem to be our place in the outer, cosmic scheme of things. The conventional rulership of the decanates (as Aries, first, Mars; Aries, second, Sun; Aries, third, Jupiter) is according to Alan Leo. This objective influence can mean both sign and decanate ruler growth of the soul.

The rulership according to Sepharial is an own inner, subjective significance. Possibly it is our own inner subjectivity that can hold us back in some way or can represent what keeps us thinking only of ourselves.

In regard to these Sepharial rulerships, be sure you note the actual placement of the rulership planet by house and sign in order to find the outlet of this subjective influence when considering any planet in your horoscope. For example, consider someone with Venus is in the third decanate of Aquarius. The Sepharial rulership is the Moon, so look to see the house and sign of the Moon. In this case the Moon is in Pisces in the third house, which is an outlet, or perhaps a cause of this subjective influence. It can concern the expression of love or a lack of ability to express the feeling nature. Even though outwardly the person may seem detached, with Venus in Aquarius there is more emotionalism than can be relayed.

You will notice how Aries is identified with Scorpio, Taurus with Sagittarius, Gemini with Capricorn, Cancer with Aquarius, and Leo with Pisces, and that Virgo stands alone. These combinations and their associated relationships could be karmic or have heavy psychic or spiritual links. In other words, these relationships affect them in a very personal, sometimes hurtful, manner.

Definition of House Affairs

The interpretation of the decanates on the cusps of the twelve houses is in relationship to the affairs of the house. The definition of the dwad on the cusp of each of the twelve houses relates to the affairs of the house. Keep in mind the nature of any planet involved with the house and adapt it to the decanate and dwad meaning.

If you have an interception in your chart, read that sign for all three decanate interpretations: physical, mental, and spiritual. The interception is a more complete influence of the sign involved, more evolved and perfected. Although it is an influence seemingly subservient to the cusp sign, its influence in the background is full and potent, more total than any single decànate influence could be, cusp-wise. The interception is a very integrated vibration of the sign.

House	Affairs
First	Personality, physical body, self-awareness, how others see you at first, early life.
Second	Resources and finances that are self-earned; what you value.
Third	Brother, sister, environment, mental interests, writing, communicating, short trips, conscious mind.
Fourth	Home, nurturing parent, conditions at close of life, how you see yourself, your cosmic connection.
Fifth	Children, love affairs, self-expression through creative work, entertainment, gambling, subjective attachments.
Sixth	Working conditions, health, clothing, employees, service to others, small animals.
Seventh	Partners, conditions in marriage, open enemies, how you see others, way to attain balance.
Eighth	Partner's income, methods of rejuvenation, inheritance, sex, death, the occult or things mysterious.
Ninth	Religion, philosophical views, advanced education, long trips, publishing, legal affairs, how you understand.
Tenth	Authoritative or dominant parent, public status, reputation, vocation, ambitions.
Eleventh	Friends, hopes and wishes, clubs and organizational work, politics, causes, objective or platonic attachments.
Twelfth	Hospitalization or confinement, self-doubt or undoing, secret trials, hidden enemies, psychic experience, karma, past life, large animals, subconscious mind.

Planet	Influence
Sun	Ego, individuality, relations with men in woman's chart (Leo-fifth house).
Moon	Domestic urge, home, relations with women in a man's chart, mother, moods, personality, emotions, feelings (Cancer-third house; Virgo-sixth house).
Mercury	Communication with others, conscious mind, relationship to and in environment, brothers and sisters, neighbors (Gemini-third house; Virgo-sixth house).
Venus	Beauty, social relationships, love, profit, marriage, ideal woman in a man's chart, a woman's ideal femininity, artistry (Taurus-second house; Libra-seventh house). For further descriptions of Venus (ideal woman in a man's chart), look to the sign on the second and seventh cusps and aspects.

Mars	Courage, energy, passion, temper, physical activity, self-projection, ideal man in a woman's chart, a male's own image (Aries-first house). A woman's Mars by sign, house and aspects describes the ideal man, but look to her Ascendant sign and aspects to describe further the relationship which may not at first be apparent.
Jupiter	Religious and philosophical drive, the desire to expand viewpoint and growth, luck, long travels, objective awareness (Sagittarius-ninth house).
Saturn	Safety urge, where fear is, self-discipline and responsibility, ambition, duty, sign of Saturn is the lesson to be learned, the father figure (Capricorn-tenth house).
Uranus	Independence of action and thought, place where we become enlightened or awakened, where we need to break free, capacity for genius, unconventional, originality, creative thinking, unexpected and sudden happenings (Aquarius-eleventh house).
Pluto	Where we rebuild or rejuvenate, secrecy, work that is pressured, death, sex, disappearance, where things may be taken in order to be replaced with something better for our growth, where things are hidden, later to be unmasked (Scorpio-eighth house).
S. Node	Talents known or already developed, also where karma may be brought to present life, where little effort is required, where the flow goes out, scattering and spreading to the many. Similar to Mars and Saturn.
N. Node	Talents where growth and new learning take place, where focalization is necessary, where great effort is needed. Similar to Venus and Jupiter.

Chapter 4

House Interpretation

These decanate interpretations are for charts with no intercepted signs. Use them as a starting point, adding your own ideas and insights.

Aries-Aries, First Decanate, 0-10°, Physical

Aries-Aries Ascendant

First House: This gives intense activity and should be used constructively. Risk-takers, they need to take precautions to prevent accidents because their energy can be used in pursuit of daredevil experiences. They tend to be loners.

Second House: This can bring income resulting from much exertion of energy. Money does not last as they do not know how to handle it. They need to not only learn how to make money but how to budget. Self-employment may be best for them.

Third House: Their thinking is impulsive, and there may be a lot of activity with brothers and sisters, or a lot of arguments with them. They exchange ideas with neighbors, which may or may not be accepted by either party.

Fourth House: They have a domineering parent and because of that are strong masters of their own homes. This position forces them to learn to relate to a parent; if unsuccessful, it can lead to revolt against family tradition. But family activities can also be warm and comforting.

Fifth House: There is much activity with children. These people are learning about personal love and selfishness involving love, as well as the art of self-expression and how best to express their creativity.

Sixth House: There is much energy that can be put to good use in work or service requiring great physical expenditure. They learn to take care of their health at an early age and can become absorbed in this task most of their lives.

Seventh House: These people learn to associate with a partner and to understand what partnerships are all about. They need to learn to adjust to the partner's desires and to strive for balance in relationships. When they find a partner, they find themselves.

Eighth House: These people need to learn to adjust to the partner's influence and attitudes concerning finances and sex. They sometimes learn the hard way that the partner must be considered where sex is concerned, and not just themselves. Time alone is rejuvenating.

Ninth House: Long-distance travel is of interest, and they learn to broaden themselves and become more objective. They are actively involved in some form of religion or philosophy in association with a more collective way of life, and can be spiritual leaders.

Tenth House: This can indicate friction with authority figures. These people could pursue a career in mechanics, engineering, the military, or a profession connected with driving. A leadership outlet is important, and they can be business pioneers in a new kind of venture.

Eleventh House: This is all about learning the art of friendship, and to express a desire or wish and go after it. They needs to control a tendency to argue with friends and the desire to be first. These people can initiate a cause or humanitarian endeavor.

Twelfth House: They need to learn to sacrifice themselves for something, to learn compassion and grasp the realization that other people suffer too. There is a drive to prove their fearlessness.

Aries-Leo, Second Decanate, 10-20°, Mental

Aries-Leo Ascendant
First House: They want to come first because they want to be applauded for what they do. They love their children and want to show them off as a reflection of themselves. Fun and drama are enjoyable, and they're quite charming.

Second House: These people are easily frustrated if finances don't go according to plan. Work is a main focus, primarily because of earning power. But a job also must allow the freedom to create because it is an ego investment for these people.

Third House: Their minds are active and they enjoy sharing their ideas. They may be community leaders, and involved with children. Thinking is a main focus, and this is more successful if they have someone, especially a partner, with whom to share their thoughts.

Fourth House: These people are interested in domestic affairs, and some become foster parents because they have a great interest in helping and teaching children. However, they can be somewhat shy. This placement can give a vigorous sex life into old age.

Fifth House: These people pursue the good life and have creative ideas and activities, which some pursue with great intensity. Much pleasure is associated with this placement, along with education and travel, and they are often ardent lovers.

Sixth House: Mental activity is more discriminating and analytical. Hard workers, they work best alone because they are task-oriented and excel at organization. They dislike taking orders, but can make a name for themselves in their chosen field.

Seventh House: Friendship can trigger arguments with a marriage partner even though these people greatly dislike conflict. The spark is often because the seventh house individual sticks up for his or her rights, and possibly the rights of the friends.

Eighth House: These people must learn to bring love into a sexual relationship. The intensity with this position should be used to create something that will bring profit to both partners. It gives a subconscious drive for dominance in a leadership position.

Ninth House: This influence indicates enthusiastic leadership in religion and subjects of the higher mind. Love can force them to open their minds to more objective thinking, which will enable them to better know themselves and others. They feel as though they have a special mission to fulfill.

Tenth House: This position gives great mental stimulation in the vocational area, and some people become egotistical because of their success. They have great dramatic ability and some are entertainers, while others easily sway the public in connection with business matters.

Eleventh House: They get to know the right people and take pride in testing their ideas with friends. This influence also gives a strong desire for approval from friends, people in the community, coworkers, and supervisors. They can be leaders in community or neighborhood groups.

Twelfth House: Their motives are intense but hidden from others, and they do a lot of soul-searching. These people are often the power behind the throne. Time alone for quiet activities and thought, especially in their own home, is their path to regular renewal.

Aries-Sagittarius, Third Decanate, 20-30°, Spiritual

Aries-Sagittarius Ascendant

First House: This position gives great optimism and enthusiasm as well as a good sense of humor. But there is a tendency to scatter energy, which is best used for higher education rather than adventurous escapades. The image they project is up to them.

Second House: Generous with their resources, they are excessively so with good causes. There is also a tendency to spend excessively. However, the more they give, the more they seem to get, as the universe often returns their largesse many times over.

Third House: These people spread news in the community and are the first in the neighborhood to be aware of any situation. They enjoy sharing news and gossip, and some organize neighbors or community members into groups for positive activities.

Fourth House: Family and domestic life are active, with people coming and going, and family members involved in many activities. The religious or philosophical influence of the family can be pervasive and extend into adulthood. Some, however, discard these beliefs.

Fifth House: These people are hard to tie down simply because they like to spread love around. Restless energy may be used for pleasurable adventures and hobbies. Natural promoters, they make good athletic coaches and trainers, and can be leaders in activities associate with children.

Sixth House: These people need a job where they can move about or travel, as well as one where they do not feel like they're just one of the crowd. They desire a high salary, and are not interested in a mundane job unless it will lead to a much bigger one.

Seventh House: These people need to learn to understand themselves and their desires as they relate to partnerships. Freedom in a relationship is vital in order to maintain well-being, and they are happiest when matched with someone who is also interested in an active lifestyle.

Eighth House: These people have a strong interest in what life after death, and there could be a strong interest in religion prior to this. Sexuality is strong but stems from a spiritual drive rather than from a purely physical one. Many engage in philosophical discussions and research.

Ninth House: Prophets of the future, these people can often sense what is coming and foresee trends. This influence endows leadership in pioneering philosophies, which are often directed toward the welfare of children or people of other cultures.

Tenth House: This influence gives executive talent, and many of these people are able to reach the top because they are hard workers who are willing to project and use their energy to its fullest. They work tirelessly to achieve a goal, and could have an aptitude for the legal field.

Eleventh House: These people are leaders in humanitarian movements, and they also have great integrity in relationships. They are artistic and inspiration comes from working on creative projects with a partner. Many take long trips with friends.

Twelfth House: These people need to let go and let a higher spiritual power take over. They sense that sex is a process of rejuvenation and that it has a connection with life and death. Some work behind the scenes for religious and humanitarian causes.

Taurus-Taurus, 0-10°, First Decanate, Physical

Taurus-Taurus Ascendant

First House: These people are either lazy or stubbornly determined; there is no in-between with them. Sensuous and pleasant until provoked, they are exceptionally loyal to loved ones and others in their inner circle.

Second House: Stubbornly determined in their drive to make money, these people are inflexible and conservative with their resources. Some are thrifty, and others are penny-pinchers. Slowly but surely, they build savings and investments.

Third House: These people are often shy and timid in communication, yet they enjoy talking siblings and neighbors they know. They are extremely stubborn in their thinking, and it's difficult to convince them to accept new ideas. Once convinced, however, they stand firm.

Fourth House: Opinions cannot be changed by family members, but cooperation out of love can encourage them to adapt. They are stubborn regarding domestic affairs, and expect everything to be just as they wish it. Anything new, once placed, remains there forever.

Fifth House: Once given, devotion to another is almost impossible to undo. They are too fixed to be exceptionally creative. This position gives great loyalty to children and loved ones because one of their important values is love and its expression.

Sixth House: These people work very hard in their strong drive to achieve financial security. As a result, they usually gain substantial wealth. But their health may suffer because of over-work, and they may have throat trouble or ulcers.

Seventh House: These people tend to be stingy in close relationships, or their partners are that way. They need to learn to adapt in favor of others. However, they can be extremely devoted in a deep relationship that once established will be a lasting one.

Eighth House: These people can be too possessive in partnerships and many are excessively and unrealistically jealous. There can be great concern and interest in the partners's money, or vice versa. A sensuous nature enhances their sex life.

Ninth House: Stubborn and fixed ideas about religion and philosophy usually stay with these people throughout their lives. Love, not force, has the power to change their views about anything, and this also could be achieved through education. They rarely jump to conclusions.

Tenth House: These people have much determination to make money through a career, and are not interested in any position unaccompanied by money and public acceptance. Only then will they work harder than anyone else. They excel at making something out of nothing.

Eleventh House: Possessive with friends, these people are more than likely to attract those who have money; but friends are not necessarily generous. They may give more to friends than they receive from them, and there can be financial involvement with humanitarian causes.

Twelfth House: With this influence there is a hidden insecurity about finances, and a subconscious feeling of being unprotected causes them much worry about having sufficient resources. They may seem flexible and free-wheeling, but in reality they hide their deep feelings from others.

Taurus-Virgo, 10-20°, Second Decanate, Mental

Taurus-Virgo Ascendant
First House: This influence gives determination to serve others in a practical manner. However, these people can struggle with active participation in the world until motivated by the love of a friend, family member, or partner. They are creative rather than critical.

Second House: These people are discriminating in their job choice. However, once in the correct job, they can be tireless workers. Their perfectionist tendencies may bother coworkers, but they will produce excellent output.

Third House: There is a focus on the environment or neighborhood, resulting in struggle or conflict. These people can be too analytical with partners if they become frustrated with the people around them. They need to learn to consider all ideas and to accept other views.

Fourth House: These people can be stubborn and critical with their families. They emphasize perfection within the domestic scene and push family members to work, work, work for money, money, money. This can indicate sexual problems, but if these people are sexually fulfilled, their drive for work and money eases.

Fifth House: These people tend to analyze and criticize children or others they love. They enjoy discussion, but their fixed, detailed nature doesn't give others much of a chance to speak. They are best when using their analytical nature, and when away from their birth place.

Sixth House: These people are focused on health and service, and may have greater job success in fields such as health care and customer service. They rarely hesitate to offer help to others, although they can be slow yet methodical workers.

Seventh House: Mates or partners are attracted because of their money or ability to help these people make money. But they criticize their partners or friends or attract those who do the same. However, they can serve these same people tirelessly by working for or with them.

Eighth House: Sex could be problematic because these people can be either too critical or too discriminating. It also gives a practical attitude toward the partner's money or the tendency to want to control it, and there can be a deep-seated, subconscious urge for power and money.

Ninth House: These people can be very fixed in religious matters. They also may care too much about public acceptance in regard to their religious beliefs instead of following their own true selves and core life philosophy. Exposure to other cultures can widen their horizons.

Tenth House: Leadership is possible with this influence, but they also need to learn to be more flexible in career matters in order to maximize financial gain. They must focus on the job without concern regarding earnings and ego satisfaction. This is a spiritual lesson.

Eleventh House: There is an underlying inferiority complex and shyness with friends and acquaintances, and they need to learn to be more generous with people and to communicate freely. They may also attract friends who could drain them financially and mentally.

Twelfth House: They need to willingly serve others and without jealousy regarding the financial success of others or in any way criticizing them. Otherwise their health can suffer. Peaceful family and home conditions are important to these people.

Taurus-Capricorn, 20-30°, Third Decanate, Spiritual

Taurus-Capricorn Ascendant
First House: There is a strong drive and personal investment in success with this influence. These people want to present themselves as masterful and skillful and they do so through their instinctive knowledge of higher truths and higher disciplines.

Second House: There is an intense preoccupation with resources and with how to be successful in order to gain more. They may be generous with their time and talents but not their finances. Lovers of the good things life has to offer, they will not deny themselves.

Third House: This placement gives a serious mind, and no one can force an idea on these people. They can be very rigid and cool to friends and neighbors, and may appear affluent even if they are not. They are at their best when determination is focused on their community.

Fourth House: These people are conservative in money matters and within the domestic circle. There is a tendency to acquire money and things just for the sake of acquisition. Family ties are so important that they want nothing to rock the boat. However, home life is sturdy and solid.

Fifth House: Possessive with children, they are also disciplinarians, and forget to let go when their children grow up. Self-expression is practical and matter of fact, and rarely creative unless other aspects show it. There is an over-abundance of self-interest.

Sixth House: These people are either very hard workers or very lazy, and they need to curb the desire to be bossy. They definitely work hard for money, but any job must be one they enjoy and in which they can be recognized. They excel at organization.

Seventh House: Once in a committed relationship they will endure much, even suffering and hardship, in order to sustain the relationship. Their environment will do a great deal to help or hinder them in these efforts. Feelings of responsibility are high with this influence.

Eighth House: These people dread growing old and dying. They also need to curb thoughts of "this is mine and no one can have it," which causes problems with partners and their resources. Their parents may have greatly influenced them, and they treat their children the same way.

Ninth House: If religious or philosophical ideas are not practical, they are not interested. They will listen but they must personally experience these things. These people ignore things they can't change. However, love or their children can help to modify their ideas.

Tenth House: They can be generous with their time if they think it will get them further in their careers. This placement also gives the ability to stand up to hardships and hard work if they're viewed favorably. In the end, though, they will want major financial rewards.

Eleventh House: Friendship and marriage may cause financial problems, which can lead to arguments. These people do not have many friends but those that they do have are lifelong companions. Their friends may be older or more serious.

Twelfth House: A hidden drive for money and power may be their downfall. There is also a great insecurity in relation to sex partners. Yet they also know and feel that power lies in the acquisition of money and a fulfilling sex life.

Gemini-Gemini, First Decanate, 0-10°, Physical

Gemini-Gemini Ascendant
First House: Energy is scattered and thus loses some of its power and actions are taken too quickly. These people need to relax often or they become extremely nervous. They also need to learn to take deep breaths for relaxation as there is a tendency for shallow breathing.

Second House: Intuition can be used in financial matters, and siblings may hinder or help in earning money (depending upon planets in this house and aspects to them). These people are best in a job involving travel or a great deal of communication.

Third House: These people try to know everyone in their environment and are versatile and friendly to all. Their approach to neighbors and associates is through mental interests, and they are the first to share information. However, they need to learn to listen more.

Fourth House: People with this placement often move frequently. If they stay put, however, they're rarely home. There can be more than one home at the same time. Adult siblings may live in the same home, or visit each other often.

Fifth House: Communication in romantic relationships is important, but these people may not be very ardent. They also can have two dating relationships at the same. Their children are likely to be intellectual rather than emotional, the parent-child tie strongest on a mental level.

Sixth House: These people often use their intuition in the workplace. But because they use much physical and nervous energy, their health can suffer, especially the nervous system. They need to relax regularly and to emphasize deep breathing.

Seventh House: The mate is usually selected more through a logical thought process than from an emotional one. A sibling of one of the partners may be important in the marriage relationship. This influence can indicate much activity by the couple in the community.

Eighth House: Sex is more of a mental encounter than an emotional one, and they can turn it on and off through thought. They have an insatiable drive to understand the mysteries of life and death, and benefit from regularly rejuvenating themselves.

Ninth House: There is curiosity about life in faraway places, and these people would love to be world travelers. Intuition and reasoning are strong, and these people can excel as higher-education teachers. They enjoy discussing abstract subjects.

Tenth House: Unless these people have variety in their job and career, they become bored, restless, and unhappy. They make good speakers and communicate well with the public. They're also more effective when a job gives them regular contact with people.

Eleventh House: They have many friends, and overall these people excel at friendship as it is impossible for them to hold bad feelings. They attract friends that are mentally flexible, with whom they can study. This may also take many short trips with friends or groups.

Twelfth House: Trouble can come through brothers and sisters because of karma. They are good listeners and can learn much by listening to others. This influence also gives an insatiable thirst for knowledge. However, self-undoing can come when they scatter their resources.

Gemini-Libra, Second Decanate, 10-20°, Mental

Gemini-Libra Ascendant

First House: These people are seldom crude or coarse, and their friendly manner and good looks have instant appeal. Love relationships, children, or art can help them project their best, and they are usually very fair with others.

Second House: These people dislike jobs that are unrefined or unclean, or that involve dirty surroundings. They can get the most out of a job through partnership or teamwork, and the ability to use creativity in some way helps them increase income.

Third House: Communication is never direct and to the point. They try to be so fair that they lack directness, and therefore can be ineffective. However, in the midst of turmoil these people are the diplomats, the peacemakers.

Fourth House: Mental indecision occurs in family and domestic life, and these people have difficult deciding where they would be happy. Although they seem quiet and peaceful, they rarely are. Over-emphasis on the partner's income and spending is common.

Fifth House: These people dislike the responsibilities of parenting and prefer their children when they become adults. They need a partner who will give feedback on their ideas, as well as one who enhances their creative or artistic expression.

Sixth House: They enjoy having people around them when they work and are more productive when fellow employees are nearby. Peaceful surroundings are essential, and their work must have variety. Some have jobs dealing with clothing, decor, art, or jewelry.

Seventh House: These people want their partners to share their emotions but are not always able to return it. They can be verbally expressive even though their heart isn't always in it. A congenial mate is a must, but they are more diplomatic in business associations.

Eighth House: There can be mental indecision regarding a sex partner, and even promiscuity. Unrest comes from the subconscious, which seems karmic. Financial gain can come through a partner; however, finances can fluctuate. There can be karmic or hidden conditions in marriage.

Ninth House: These people promote justice because their higher minds can be impartial and fair. Their thinking broadens as they become older, and they make decisions without emotion. They can be excellent and persuasive orators, but worry about the impression they make.

Tenth House: In the workplace these people are at their best working with partners—people with whom they can discuss problems. They are more successful in careers that involve communication, and are fair and diplomatic. In partnership they can and do make money.

Eleventh House: They can build consensus within groups, and are also diplomats and peace-makers among the friends in their circle. Leaders in social groups, clubs, and organizations, they can excel in public relations as they are keenly aware of trends.

Twelfth House: Indecisiveness stems from weak self-esteem. These people are restless and feel uncomfortable in unfamiliar environments. Even when they appear to be at peace with the outside world, subconscious emotions are a strong force in their lives.

Gemini-Aquarius, Third Decanate, 20-30°, Spiritual

Gemini-Aquarius Ascendant
First House: Errands, quick trips, and travel promote health because these activities help minimize nervous tension. They need plenty of exercise even though they seem physically strong. This position gives an inquisitive mind in search of intellectual truths.

Second House: Income can come through anything classified as scientific or electrical, from research to engineering to appliance sales. Money comes more easily when they're objective about it and not obviously seeking it, and they may have more than one job.

Third House: These people are original thinkers and writers, and when they realize the facts of a situation, they want to impart this knowledge. They feel everyone has a right to know the truth. Restlessness aids the search for information and encourages independence.

Fourth House: Restless to the core of their being, these people like to move from place to place. They rebel against tradition, sometimes radically so, and renew themselves through liberal ideas. They are not hampered by the crystallized opinions that keep others in bondage.

Fifth House: The head rules romance, and their priority is to stay free. Beneath it all they remain cool and detached. They communicate well with children, teaching and helping with detachment. Rebellious at times, they are unconventional or individualistic.

Sixth House: These people are at their best in a job with the freedom to diversify, move about, and use their creative minds. Communication with many is also important in order to avoid frustration. They are ingenious in finding ways to make money.

Seventh House: They look for intellect in a partner or someone who is unconventional and original. The freedom to have other close friends is also important, especially those that enhance communication and the exchange of ideas in order to broaden their minds.

Eighth House: These conventional people can be independent and original regarding sex. Ideas may arise more out of curiosity than passion. They believe in self-regeneration through knowledge of their world and the universe. Some are unconventional parents or grew up with one.

Ninth House: These people not only want to learn new things but want to broadcast them to all who will listen. They search for religious truth using logic and reason and are quick to challenge views that differ from their own. Then their actions mirror their views.

Tenth House: They need a job where they can mingle and discuss issues and ideas in a teamwork atmosphere. The desire to work with many people is stronger than the kind of work they do, and their original ideas can benefit all coworkers in the workplace.

Eleventh House: Their friends are never dull, and they dislike boring people. They rarely welcome coworkers into their circle of friendship. Highly social and outgoing, they usually have many friends in common with a partner.

Twelfth House: Conscious thoughts cannot always be linked to everyday experiences, and at times they seem to be driven by subconscious promptings. However, this gives them spiritual objectivity and a mind open to learning the mysteries of life.

Cancer-Cancer, First Decanate, 0-10°, Physical

Cancer-Cancer Ascendant
First House: These people project themselves with caution out of fear of being hurt. They know how it feels and therefore they tend to be over-protective of loved ones. Activity is often sporadic, occurring only when pushed by others. These people tend to gain weight.

Second House: This influence indicates financial successful because they know what the public wants. They play on the emotions of the people in order to increase their own assets. Usually unemotional, they do not squander their money, but this fluctuates.

Third House: These people are sensitive to the environment, and usually do not like to studying. This changes when a teacher touches their emotions; then they excel, quickly absorbing knowledge. Family members nearby add to their contentment.

Fourth House: These people over-idealize their childhood or one parent. This position also indicates restlessness, which makes encourages frequent relocation or changes within the home. They seem to long for the childhood they cannot again experience.

Fifth House: These people are emotional, sentimental, and vulnerable in love and romance, and it also encourages they to be tenacious and clinging with loved ones. Sensitive about their children, they have strong instincts concerning them. Some are exceptionally creative.

Sixth House: The workplace may seem like a second home, and they may treat coworkers or employees like part of their family. These people can be obsessive about nutrition and what they and their family eat. Uncontrolled emotions can cause illness.

Seventh House: A woman with this aspect will tend to mother her mate; a man wants a wife who will mother him. There is an emotional attitude concerning marriage, even the Capricorn influence makes them seem cold and unsympathetic. Financial gain may be a primary motive for marriage.

Eighth House: These people may seem free and easy, but there is an underlying emotional concern about life after death. However, when deeply involved with someone, they pull back in order to ponder the relationship. They are often aggressive, going after what they want.

Ninth House: These people develop an emotional attachment with their location even if far from home. They have deep, penetrating feelings about religion and ethics, and emotion plays a big part in their exploration and adoption of a religious beliefs.

Tenth House: These people sense what others want and do well because they cater to the desires of the public. However, they can also hop from job to job. Popularity is usually high, with others seeking their attention, opinions, and influence.

Eleventh House: Friends are viewed as part of their family, and they have strong emotional connections with them and can be easily hurt. This position may cause the people to act as parent figures to friends, who are encouraged to congregate in their homes.

Twelfth House: These people have deep emotions but usually keep them to themselves. Dreamers whose big dreams seldom come true, they are generous but feel badly when those they love do not appreciate their gestures. However, they rarely express these feelings.

Cancer-Scorpio, Second Decanate, 10-20°, Mental

Cancer-Scorpio Ascendant
First House: This decanate gives physical endurance, and they can endure more emotional strain. They are secretive, mysterious, and proud, and are apt to express anger when something goes wrong with a relationship or their children.

Second House: No one ever knows exactly how much money these people make, which is often considerable. Yet they maintain tight budgets—except for domestic items—because they fear financial insecurity. They work hard, primarily to maximize income.

Third House: At times they can be blunt in speech, especially with partners or relatives. They also have fixed opinions, and thus there can be many arguments with loved ones over finances. But they also can be financially successful in partnership with another.

Fourth House: Very interested in family, they have a stable and permanent home life. They have strong ideas concerning domestic matters and expect all in the home to accept them. No one outside the family will learn much about their home life, however.

Fifth House: Sentimental and romantic, behind all exterior displays there runs the thrill of seeking forbidden love. If they turn this drive toward a creative project, it can alleviate the tendency for self-suffering in love. Religion may be a reason romance doesn't work out.

Sixth House: These people become so involved with work that the workplace verges on being a second home. They are attached to the people they work for and with, and if they can turn this deep need into the study of psychology or social work, it can become a satisfying career.

Seventh House: They have deep, possessive feelings for partners and friends, and may keep secrets from those they love. Loyal, protective, and sympathetic, partnerships endure even when relationships change. They bring a strong sexuality to love, and are possessive in close relationships.

Eighth House: Their passion is sensuous, but they will never talk about sexual intimacy. Generally honest, they do not talk about problems and tend to keep everything inside. Some, however, substitute with a drive for money and possessions that brings no real satisfaction.

Ninth House: These people have deep mental powers that when controlled and directed can help them solve the mysteries of existence. Meditation is beneficial. They learn best through experience rather than academics, and project strength to others.

Tenth House: Along with a talent for sensing the needs/desires of the public is one for delving into the secrets of nature itself. This can give a successful career dealing with the public. They sense many things concerning their careers and thus may take less obvious avenues to success.

Eleventh House: These people help friends as long as friends don't let them down. However, close friends are few in number. Some are protective, sympathetic neighborhood parents, and they know all about their neighbors even though neighbors don't really know them.

Twelfth House: Deep within they want to be loved and nurtured. Although outwardly extroverted, they hide their sensitivity and any hurts that occur. This can indicate a subconscious complex regarding sex, love, and/or the partner's money, if married.

Cancer-Pisces, Third Decanate, 20-30°, Spiritual

Cancer-Pisces Ascendant
First House: These people are spiritual and self-sacrificing with a strong need to be nurtured. They are consciously aware that their mother influence is instinctively with them, but their goals seem to remain hidden. They desire to learn the eternal truths.

Second House: These people can make money through their innate knowledge of what the public wants and needs because they can tune in to their emotions. They spend on dreams and schemes that may or may not work out, but can do well in a Pisces influenced career.

Third House: Aware of hidden influences within the environment or hidden meanings behind what people say, these people seek this information but keep their feelings to themselves. They seek friendships where they can talk about life without others asking personal information.

Fourth House: Willing to make great sacrifices for the family, these people never seem to be able to forget the past and are driven by subconscious urges to discover their deeper identities. This discovery can come through religion, the occult, the study of reincarnation, and researching their family tree.

Fifth House: These people often get what they want because they act on instinct. They are willing to sacrifice for love and the creativity that goes with it, and can express their sentimental feelings. They can be romantic in both words and actions, sacrificing when necessary.

Sixth House: These people may not work excessively hard, but because they like money they will maneuver as necessary, sometimes behind the scenes, in order to be successful. They are tenacious and hold onto a job, but fluctuate between being lazy and active.

Seventh House: They need friends and sympathetic marriage partners with whom to discuss their problems, and in turn can make great sacrifices for others. These may be the people who sacrifice marriage to care for an aged or sick relative, or to pursue some noble cause.

Eighth House: These people rejuvenate themselves by going to a special place within their home and locking themselves away until they feel revived. They can sublimate their passions and sex drives, if necessary. There may be confusion with an inheritance or with a marriage partner's money.

Ninth House: These people ultimately need to know the reason for their existence, and love motivates them to study higher truths and philosophy. They understand self-sacrifice in religion and in their pursuit of higher knowledge. Their minds are very creative and imaginative.

Tenth House: These people know instinctively what people want and thus gravitate to and excel in careers where they can use this ability such as working with the public in some capacity. Hard work brings them financial rewards, which is how they measure their success in life.

Eleventh House: Sympathetic with friends, they take great pains and devote much time to try to understand their problems. But they're seldom as generous with their money, even with loved ones. However, they will leave what could be substantial legacies for their favorite causes.

Twelfth House: These people have great pride and if successful financially they are happy, outgoing, and well-adjusted. However, they suffer family problems in silence. There may be problems with a partner and finances because either person is too conservative or greatly lacks generosity.

Leo-Leo, First Decanate, 0-10°, Physical

Leo-Leo Ascendant

First House: These people are sunshine itself (or think they are), and have a tendency to overdo it in many activities. At first they appear arrogant, but this is many times a facade for they are truly warmhearted. They are often physically attractive in a vital, dramatic way.

Second House: These people want to make money, and satisfy their egos by accumulating objects so friends will marvel. Many times these objects will increase in value. Their egos are also gratified when their children do well financially. They enjoy entertaining friends.

Third House: They communicate ideas with a dramatic flair and are charismatic with an instinct for knowing just what to say. These are the people in the community or neighborhood that everyone knows. They are loving and somewhat possessive of brothers and sisters.

Fourth House: Their homes are lavish, places for entertaining others in grand style. They also want recreational items in the home, such as a swimming pool, pool table, or high-end electronics, and are usually viewed as the lords of their home of their neighborhood.

Fifth House: Pleasure can dominate their lives. They have great physical energy, which should be directed into constructive creativity. But they tend to dominate those they love and are very proud and make good friends but poor enemies. They can be excellent actors.

Sixth House: They need to love their work, which should give them the freedom to create, and they also take great pride in their work if they like what they're doing. If not, dramatics ensue, especially if they feel a task is beneath them. They work best with a partner.

Seventh House: The ego must shine through, with, and in marriage. They must be proud of the partner, and need love in marriage. Even though they want to dominate, chances are they partner will want to dominate them. Trust and freedom in commitment are of utmost importance.

Eighth House: These people have good financial and business instincts, and when they direct their energy there, they can achieve great ambitions. They thrive on big investments, and make good sex partners because they know how to combine the emotions with physical stimulation.

Ninth House: This position gives extreme confidence in ideas, which they go to great lengths to express. They want to enlighten everyone and truly believe in love. When they want to relax, they enjoy long vacation trips and other outdoor recreational activities.

Tenth House: Ambitious and driven, their tremendous talent for self-expression can help them make a name for themselves in the business world. The drive for ego satisfaction is best served when expressing and communicating ideas, if not on a broad scale, then within the community.

Eleventh House: Friends are given the royal treatment, but they also choose their friends with care and are quite proud of these relationships. But they also expect their own light to shine through what their friends do. Many of these people promote cultural activities in the community.

Twelfth House: These people are the power behind the throne, driven by a subconscious desire for dominance or leadership, yet feeling more or less unappreciated. The marriage partner experiences the brunt of this, or they may develop open enemies with whom they express their frustrated leadership potential.

Leo-Sagittarius, Second Decanate, 10-20°, Mental

Leo-Sagittarius Ascendant

First House: Activities must have an ideal or a purpose behind them, such as education for children or a religious, philosophical, or scientific advancement that will somehow benefit many people. Most of these people are worthy of trust placed in them because they have great integrity.

Second House: These people are financially optimistic and also have integrity in this area. They drive themselves to be high earners, always in an ethical manner, because of love, their children, or their creativity. They also have visions regarding earning power that extend far into the future.

Third House: These people communicate the broad view in an optimistic, enthusiastic manner. Others listen to them. But they can get on the soap box, espousing religious theory or philosophy because of their beliefs instead of in an attempt to change others. Their ability to serve and work for others is endless.

Fourth House: Morals guide these people, especially in their domestic and family lives, where integrity is of utmost importance, even in disagreements. They also want homes that are bigger and better than what they have or that someone else has. Although sex drive is strong, it subconsciously relates to carrying on the family.

Fifth House: These people are gamblers with everything from money to relationships to their ambitions. When they sacrifice for and believe in loved ones, and put them above themselves, they are magnificent and make excellent teachers and counselors. They bring enthusiasm and understanding to education.

Sixth House: This influences gives a capacity for working long hours and for seeing long-range commitments. Employment isn't just employment; they have a career in mind. The view is toward the future, and they can labor long hours with optimism and enthusiasm to achieve their goals.

Seventh House: These people sometimes shy away from commitment in relationships. If they do achieve this, however, it is because there is much friendship and communication involved. They need a partner with whom they can share ideas because partnership is all about love and comradery.

Eighth House: Even though these people enjoy the physical pleasures of life with much zest, they have a supreme belief in life beyond death. Deep religious faith seems to come from a past of which they may not be exactly aware, and within them is a love that values the deep, enduring beauty of a spiritual bond.

Ninth House: These people have a natural promotional ability, and even though they believe wholeheartedly in their own ideas, they are broad-minded about others. Inspired by instinct and knowledge, their thoughts can be prophetic, and their intuition is often very accurate.

Tenth House: Long-distance travel may be connected with the career. These people also have great integrity and honesty in their work and in earning money. They eventually earn large incomes, but more important is that their work leave a lasting legacy. They pursue their dreams.

Eleventh House: These people attract friends from other cultures, and they are gregarious and enjoy exchanging views. They have large circle of friends or are involved in large social organizations. Close friends are usually very talented in some way or another.

Twelfth House: These people are clever and usually one step ahead of everyone else. There is a subconscious drive for intellectual supremacy, and they take tremendous pride in domestic affairs. They also have great integrity regarding the family. However, there also may be secrets regarding a family member.

Leo-Aries, Third decanate, 20-30°, Spiritual

Leo-Aries Ascendant
First House: These people need to be first, and enjoy socializing. But when things get rough, they take off in search of a more pleasant gathering. They can be arrogant, depending upon other aspects in the chart, and ego-gratification impresses them and builds support.

Second House: These people enjoy making a grand display and thus often spend too much, resulting in depleted finances. They have good earning power and work hard, investing their tremendous energy. Some are entertainers, and most are leaders in the workplace.

Third House: These people have something to say, and they say it. They have the ability to convince others of almost anything, and many are story-tellers because they want to communicate and entertain. Some excel as speakers, lecturers, or journalists.

Fourth House: To the public these people are diplomatic and friendly, but at home they can be argumentative and domineering. They have a subconscious need to show their fearlessness and take risks and push themselves to the limits in order to prove this.

Fifth House: They are ardent, affectionate, and demonstrative in love affairs, and enjoy dramatic moments with loved ones, including their children, and expect praise in return. Enthusiastic about sports, they are often excellent athletes. Courage and willpower encourage them to attempt almost anything.

Sixth House: These people are hard workers because deep within they believe they have a special mission in life. They are often better working for themselves and being their own boss, because this enhances their initiative, drive, and earning power.

Seventh House: They need others to share their pride in the marriage partner as this satisfies their strong ego. They are original in their ideas and expressions and seem relatively independent and free to people who do not know them well. But they can be dominated by their partner.

Eighth House: They rejuvenate themselves by staying alone at home. Often projected into financial success by an overambitious mother, they are usually successful with strong ambitions. They are usually sexually active well into their later years, sometimes with a younger partner.

Ninth House: When energy that could be expended on pleasure is instead used for higher education or philosophical pursuits, they can go far. The same applies to their innate leadership ability, which they can use to inform others as they broaden their own horizons.

Tenth House: These people need to be leaders in their careers and back up this desire with hard work. Creative challenges are also important, and they prefer solo work to teamwork. This influence especially favors work in the entertainment or with children.

Eleventh House: These people initiate new ideas, businesses, and humanitarian efforts, but other can react to them in an aggressive manner. They stimulate and motivate friends to action. However, when this influence is felt by the marriage partner, it can lead to conflict).

Twelfth House: They have a deep interest in the partner's finances. They have a drive for purity that hides their deep personal need on the physical level, and there is a struggle to turn that drive into spiritual areas. Some turn leadership into a drive for power.

Virgo-Virgo, First Decanate, 0-10°, Physical

Virgo-Virgo Ascendant
First House: These people work until a job is done correctly, exerting a great deal of energy and common sense. This results in success as a trouble-shooter. They do not stand out in a crowd, for the nature is rather modest, quiet, and shy. At their best they serve quietly and humbly.

Second House: These people know how to maintain financial and other records, and should not worry about money. If they do, their health will suffer. They have big ideas and want to make a big show and display, but even so they are willing to work to achieve their goals.

Third House: They are often too critical of the people around them, and need to learn to be more content with the way things are now and not so concerned about the future. They must guard against trying to improve other people, and can be pushy with neighbors and siblings.

Fourth House: Their health can suffer if they do not have the right place to live, and their homes must be neat and orderly. Otherwise, they are mentally out of synch. Some of these people have benefit from a job where they work out of their home.

Fifth House: Although they seem to enjoy fun and romance, they are critical of loved ones, and discriminating when choosing a mate. They want everything to be clear-cut and to know what is happening at all times. When this is impossible, they become frustrated. They do not like surprises. Good food especially pleases them.

Sixth House: These people work very hard if their work involves the use of their analytical ability. Diet is important, and they are overly concerned with caring of themselves. They need a job where freedom is not restricted, and hey criticize coworkers even though they themselves have a hard time accepting criticism.

Seventh House: These people have a tendency to criticize the partner even when there's no reason to do so. This is only the outward transference of their own feelings of inadequacy to the partner. They expect too much, and in many cases it might be better if they remained single.

Eighth House: This isn't a good position for an abundant sex life because they are too discriminating. However, in its positive vibration this can be a positive influence. Attention to detail and the ability to deal with things in an analytical fashion can be put to good use in research.

Ninth House: These people are not religious in the sense that they have unseen faith, for they are too critical. They want beliefs to be correct and perfectly sound and practical. They believe in rules and cannot move from the center to allow for differences in people and philosophy.

Tenth House: The Sagittarius Ascendant gives broad horizons, but on the job they get down to details and work hard. They want the organization they work for to be large and safe with excellent backing, and do not want to start on speculation. Any business launched will have time-tested people behind it.

Eleventh House: These people may attract critical friends who seem more unfeeling than is really true. They have only a select few friends in whom they can confide. Unless there is a strong Aries influence elsewhere in the chart they usually give in to the ideas of the group.

Twelfth House: Criticism can stem from a subconscious thoughts and messages, and these people can give too much attention to the details involved in presenting a beautiful appearance. Health problems can be difficult to diagnose, and drugs can be dangerous for people with this placement.

Virgo-Capricorn, Second Decanate, 10-20°, Mental

Virgo-Capricorn Ascendant

First House: A woman with this position may be too conscious of how she is being perceived; therefore, she is more apt to want to be safe than sorry. A man with this position will be much more sexy, being influenced by the masculine drive Capricorn gives. In other words, a man will feel this influence much more positively than a woman.

Second House: These people feel a great responsibility and may work so hard that it causes adverse health effects. They are careful with money and know where every penny goes. Generally thrifty, they will splurge on some luxury items.

Third House: These people can be uncommunicative and are usually dissatisfied with their environment. They feel restricted by the responsibility of marriage and/or their relatives, but may work hard to change conditions in the neighborhood.

Fourth House: The home is very organized and contains items that show pride in ancestral treasures. They have an exemplary reputation in the neighborhood as they believe in following the rules. Inheritance plays an important role in or with the home, such as caring for a sick parent.

Fifth House: These people are disciplinarians with their children. In their self-expressions they like to discuss philosophy or religion, and their children are probably well trained in the family religion. They do need much love even though it may seem otherwise. However, they are warmer with those with whom they have a mental connection.

Sixth House: They work hard and have great ambitions to go higher up the ladder. They can be impatient, but still do the job well and never let impatience interfere with their work. Best as supervisors or in leadership positions, they make excellent coordinators.

Seventh House: They may marry a friend, or the relationship with the marriage partner may turn into a friendship. Some have a conservative marriage relationship. They have the same friends, who are considerably important to both of them. A mutual friend may have introduced them.

Eighth House: They think everything is obtained through the mind and should learn that they also need love. They can be critical of the partner in sex or can pull back because of lack of warmth. There may be criticism because of the partner's income, and there is a subconscious drive for power.

Ninth House: Matters associated with religion and philosophy must have a material and practical benefit. They may travel, but usually only for business reasons. They have a legalistic approach to religion and are usually orthodox, and discourage others from making waves where religion is concerned.

Tenth House: These are the people who can organize anything, and at the same time fulfill a deep need to serve. However, they also want power. They need to give the world something, and should not make themselves greater than the purpose they serve. They can straighten out complicated business situations.

Eleventh House: They are at their best when the drive to serve and work is centered on a humanitarian cause or friends. But they are usually the ones who do not easily relate with others. They take life too seriously, and need to learn to laugh more with their companions.

Twelfth House: There are strong karmic ties with the family and as a result these people may tirelessly serve a parent or the entire family. They can be inwardly critical, and need to learn to serve others with understanding and compassion. Their way is not necessarily the only right way.

Virgo-Taurus, Third Decanate, 20-30°, Spiritual

Virgo-Taurus Ascendant
First House: To be their best they need to surrender to a religious conviction or develop their knowledge through ongoing education. This is the way to diminish their inferiorities. When they are sure of their education and the service they give others, they can be more loving and creative and thus lose their need to criticize.

Second House: This gives the ability for hard work in order to achieve financial success, and many attract a large amount of money. Critical regarding earnings, they look for better ways to make more. They attract money but they can use it lavishly if their hearts are involved.

Third House: These people are tireless workers in the community, the ones willing to serve causes, especially those initiated by friends and those involving fundraising. They also may be the ones who criticize siblings but always in the interest of improving them.

Fourth House: There is a secret drive for dominance and power. They take their families too seriously, and make take their desire for perfection out on their families. Behind all outward experiences is the will to make money so that they can be accepted by others.

Fifth House: These people can be stubborn and critical as a romance grows. However, in love they want to serve and help the beloved in some way. They may take a back seat in preference to a mate, but they are nearly always operating as a backseat driver, directing things from behind.

Sixth House: The influence with this position is to work hard for money, and these people can be stubborn and fixed in connection with their health and working conditions. They are interested in a correct diet and almost fanatical about it, and feel the same about the job environment.

Seventh House: This can be a partnership with two people earning joint income, or it can be working together in a job involving communication, travel, teaching, or any of the mercurial talents. Criticism can result when one is not doing a good enough job or when not enough money is coming in.

Eighth House: These people are fussy about sexual encounters and critical of the partner's financial contribution. Financially stubborn and conservative in family matters, their outgoing nature does not necessarily extend to home life or the role as parent, but they can be surprisingly sensuous.

Ninth House: These people are open-minded with religion and philosophy, and often work within the community with young people. But they are not as flexible as they seem. The ability to sort out correct and pertinent facts and to organize procedures makes them sought after for projects.

Tenth House: This gives the ability to back up ambition with work, and the innate knowledge of how to organize things in order to make money. They have one-track minds and acquire resources almost without limit. They go right to the point with their Sagittarius Ascendant.

Eleventh House: This influence attracts partnerships and friends who will be critical, and there is a need here for friends who are the opposite. There is usually a question of money for or with partners or friends. Generally, they are a stingy with friends, or friends are stingy with them.

Twelfth House: Their health suffers from over-emphasis of problems related to the partner's finances. Either there is a lack of or tightness with money. Part of the concern with money could be health treatment of the mate, the individual, or a family member.

Libra-Libra, First Decanate, 0-10°, Physical

Libra-Libra Ascendant
First House: Because they want to be liked by everyone, they tend to agree too easily. They dislike being alone, and usually can't take a stand because they want peace and want to be fair. However, another type can't do anything without getting many people on their side. They find themselves when they find their partners.

Second House: They work best at making money with a partner; however, at times they may not work as hard as the partner. They dislike working alone. Money is spent on possessions that have artistic beauty. Their job needs to leave them feeling neat, clean, and at peace.

Third House: These people need to have peaceful and beautiful surroundings. They usually entertain a lot, and some are matchmakers. Although they dislike arguing, they are excellent at debate. They often attract freedom-loving friends and partners.

Fourth House: These people needs a partner to live with in an artfully decorated home. The partner will have a conservative tendency, and these people will share the mate's high ambitions. A woman may choose a partner who treats her like a father would. If a man, he will choose someone to mother him.

Fifth House: These people like to socialize and enjoy fun, games, and amusements. They do not like doing leisure-time activities by themselves. Charming to all, they may have more than one love affair at the same time. They need for others to respond to their charms.

Sixth House: These are the people who settle workplace differences and fight for fair treatment for all. In the end, however, they may incur the enmity of management. They are also overall more interested in relationships and partnerships than is typical of Aries.

Seventh House: Partners are viewed in terms of themselves with is not always favorable for relationships. These people thus need to curb a tendency to try to influence a partner's ideas and behavior. When this is overcome and balance is learned, they reach a high level of sharing.

Eighth House: Financial success seems tied to the partner, and there is a tendency for it to fluctuate. If they work hard and restrain the tendency to criticize the partner, there can be real financial and spiritual growth for both. They also must learn to share resources.

Ninth House: They listen to everyone's philosophy and believe in true equality. After being exposed to all sides, they come to the truth in a fair and unbiased way and can in turn teach these truths in an easy manner. However, they tend to attract marriage partners who dominate them, or vice versa.

Tenth House: In business these people often work with partners. Fair with their associates, they believe in the cause of justice and thus make excellent judges and lawyers, and can be successful in any career that benefits from a talent for arbitration. They are outstanding diplomats.

Eleventh House: These people either marry a friend or a marriage partner turns into a friend, and they usually have good social lives. They need to make set and follow through on their life goals, which can be influenced by friends. If they achieve goals, it is likely to be those encouraged by friends rather than their own.

Twelfth House: There is karma connected with marriage or partnerships. Promptings seem to come from the subconscious or from patterns from another lifetime. This is corrected or helped through sacrificial service given for the true soul partner rather than for selfish interests.

Libra-Aquarius, Second Decanate, 10-20°, Mental

Libra-Aquarius Ascendant

First House: They project charm, sociability, and a desire to please people. Even so, they retain independence. In love they are ruled by their minds rather than their hearts. Most are creative. While they need partners to enhance personal success, they have a tendency to fluctuate between attachment and detachment.

Second House: These people promote cooperation in workplace, but will do an even better job if they can use their own ingenuity and originality. Partners can bring out their best, especially those who will adopt and participate in developing these new ideas. This can add considerably to income.

Third House: Environmental harmony is important to these people, and they're happiest when others agree with their original ideas. However, they also will debate in order to achieve understanding and support. Above all, they want others to like them and will adjust as necessary in order to gain acceptance.

Fourth House: These people are home- and family-oriented, and dislike living alone. They want a comfortable, warm, safe, and beautiful home. Their original ideas are often expressed in home decor. However, they also can have somewhat unusual ideas about sexual freedom, which has the power to rejuvenate their lives.

Fifth House: Good times with good friends are important to these people, and they enjoy discussing life philosophy and subjects of the higher mind. Although their lives are mostly conventional, they also enjoy talking about advanced ideas. They may have more friends of the opposite sex.

Sixth House: They want peaceful conditions where they work and want fairness for all and can be cooperative with management in impersonal ways. If the originality and inventiveness of their nature are used in their vocations they are at their best.

Seventh House: In partnership, these people expect others to accept them as they are, and they seek those who are lively and stimulating. They need to guard against a tendency to be abrupt in speech and to constantly remind themselves that diplomacy is necessary. Partnership relationships may begin as friendship.

Eighth House: Through a partner these people may become interested in the unknown such as the mysteries of life and death, and of conscious and subconscious thoughts. They are psychic and may communicate with unseen forces or tune in on vibrations that give them knowledge and insights.

Ninth House: It takes these people a while to establish their life philosophies, but once they do they use them to help others. When Libra is balanced and higher abstract ideas emphasized, they can remain detached and thus guide and encourage others to help themselves.

Tenth House: These people have a knack for public relations, and they work well with partners and have original, ingenious ways to earn money. Although inwardly warm, they are generally outwardly cool in dealing with others and thus are able to remain objective in decision making. Many excel in administrative work.

Eleventh House: When involved in a group endeavor, these people can bring diverse elements and opinions together in order to create consensus through persuasion. They excel at executing and sharing their own original ideas, as well as helping others to see and make the most of their potential.

Twelfth House: These people have unconventional attitudes and opinions, and there can be difficulties with family members or in partnership because they are so broad-minded. They secretly like to shock people, and some have a tendency to reveal information shared in confidence.

Libra-Gemini, Third Decanate, 20-30°, Spiritual

Libra-Gemini Ascendant
First House: These people are refined and expressive, and can talk with anyone. They can be persuasive lecturers, and they sound as though they know a great deal more than they do. This placement also enhances the ability for gesturing and clear expression in order to make a point.

Second House: Communication is an important job factor for these people who may also have more than one job at a time. Maximum success accompanies employment that allows creative or artistic expression. These people can make money through partnerships, and some achieve the same by working with siblings.

Third House: When they communicate they are never direct and to the point. They try to be too fair and therefore do not accomplish as much. These people like their environment to be peaceful and beautiful, but they also can be arbitrators. Time to socialize with friends is a must.

Fourth House: These people want a home but can't make up their minds about it. They need precisely the proper environment but can't seem to find it. Although they may seem peaceful and quiet, they are not. They have a deep subconscious dissatisfaction they cannot explain.

Fifth House: These people desire partners to relate to and with whom they can discuss information. They do not like the responsibility of handling children without partners because they need help with the decisions. Without a partner to love, they tend to scatter their energy.

Sixth House: They need people around them when they work, and peaceful surroundings are essential for them to do a good job. They are excellent if their work has variety. They have a flair for beautifying their environment or neighborhood. It is their way to be of service.

Seventh House: These people can be verbally expressive when they want to, but the heart isn't always in it. They believe in the theory of twin souls, and need sentiment from their partners but do not always give it themselves. They are much more the diplomat within the community than at home.

Eighth House: There can be great mental indecision or unrest regarding a sex partner. Unrest can come from impatience with home conditions or dislike of where they live. The financial situation can be improved by working with, or because of, a deep relationship, especially in a job related to Mercury or Venus.

Ninth House: They understand justice, and their higher minds can be impartial and fair. Their minds broaden as they age. This also gives a creative mind behind which is keen reason and logic that can take them far in the world of higher education or law.

Tenth House: They are best working with a partner or someone with whom they can discuss problems—someone who can help make decisions. They are more successful in jobs that utilize their powers of communication. Fair and diplomatic, they need working conditions that are peaceful.

Eleventh House: They can bring different groups of people together, including those who previously may have been unable to see eye-to-eye. They are the diplomats or peacemakers among the friends. These people keep groups, clubs, and organizations alive with their ideas.

Twelfth House: This indicates problems in marriage and discussions or arguments concerning finances. They should avoid deception and secrets and be open and above-board with all partners. These people may also be able to teach others about the mysteries of life.

Scorpio-Scorpio, First Decanate, 0-10°, Physical

Scorpio-Scorpio Ascendant
First House: These people have a sexual magnetism that has little to do with looks or age. They are strong, with great fortitude, and when physical strength requires heroism or determination, they have it in abundance. There is great depth and intensity. No one really knows them.

Second House: These people have a way with money, and are good with other people's money if other aspects agree. They make excellent investors or financiers. At some time in their lives a great transformation can take place regarding what they really value above all else.

Third House: They communicate with the people around them and may be charming, but few really know anything about them. They are secretive, believing that when people know too much they can use it against them. The partner's financial images are important to them and advance their status.

Fourth House: These people will never talk about the things that go on at home. There may be an element of sacrifice in caring for a parent, or a family situation that will remain a mystery to friends or the public. One parent may be possessive and possibly too strong or overpowering.

Fifth House: There is a tendency to be very passionate and jealous, and they are demanding and possessive of their children and other loved ones. They also believe in the rejuvenating effect of sex on people when they are not bound by prejudice and prudery, and some have many affairs.

Sixth House: These people have an uncanny ability to analyze what is wrong and to ferret out facts that can lead to improved working conditions. They are not talkative on the job about their personal affairs, and some are talented detectives. They are also well organized and efficient.

Seventh House: They can be jealous and possessive of partners, and they will not stray if they are satisfied sexually. They may keep secrets from their partners, but the partners must not keep secrets from them. They have a very strong moral code concerning sexual conduct in marriage.

Eighth House: They will never discuss their private affairs with anyone, and are perhaps obsessed with the sensual side of human nature and thus lose some of the spiritual side of the sexual union. This may can be a mercenary position, giving them an abnormal interest in other people's money.

Ninth House: These people are sharp in solving mysteries, and delve into abstract theories. They are excellent at getting to the center of things. But they do not like formal higher education and would rather teach themselves. They feel they have better answers, at least for them.

Tenth House: These people need a career that involves uncovering secrets, such as chemistry, investigation, psychology, and even astrology. They will not quit until a job is finished and they have the final answer. If necessary, they can deal with details, and will be more successful if they use their probing minds.

Eleventh House: They are very loyal to their friends and will defend them and keep their secrets. They become well known late in life and usually hold positions of financial prominence among their circle of friends and associates. However, not all their friends may know each other.

Twelfth House: They need to learn that sex should be associated with love, not lust. Then their subconscious complexes about sex will be corrected. They sometimes allow emotional self-indulgence to dominate their feelings. Some can develop rare insights into the occult world.

Scorpio-Pisces, Second Decanate, 10-20°, Mental

Scorpio-Pisces Ascendant

First House: They are seemingly very sure of themselves, but behind this bold exterior is a sensitive individual who sooner or later feels hurt by love. Even so, this position can endure more hurt than most. Failure spurs these people to greater heights after the hurt has subsided.

Second House: These people have a subconscious fear of loss, and because of this they are driven to work hard and make money. They never tell much they have accumulated, which stems from a fear that others may want to impose upon them. But they do like the good life and having luxuries.

Third House: These people are not very good at communicating with their associates because they may be too blunt or secretive. They can be dreamers, and much of what they do takes on a behind-the-scenes flavor. They present an image of being realistic, but are just the opposite; they gather strength from the unseen.

Fourth House: They keep family secrets to themselves, and manifest an outward pride in the family's presentation of an image of good breeding. They can feel hurt and unloved, and by refusing to say what is bothering them, they may push the family away without meaning to do so.

Fifth House: They have great creative talent, possibly in writing and music. But they can become moody when dissatisfied with their love lives. They learn more than most by watching and observing people and events. When they love they do so to the depths of their being.

Sixth House: Despite a seeming attachment and deep involvement with their jobs, there is hidden insecurity where finances are concerned. They do not want to be caught without an alternative way to make money, just in case one method fails, and thus sometimes have dual jobs.

Seventh House: They may be called upon to make certain sacrifices for the partner, who is very important to them, not only physically but emotionally and mentally. Marriage has to be right or they suffer inwardly, eventually affecting the health. A strong temper is usually well hidden.

Eighth House: They hide their more sensitive and gentle nature, and need to learn to rejuvenate themselves through sex and service to humanity. They need to learn that it is not weakness to show the more gentle part of their nature. This may be the poet who hides his or her work for fear of it appearing too sensitive.

Ninth House: Even though they are very psychic and can understand and learn the truths of the universe, they never lose their own identities in the conscious, material world. The more evolved they are the more they attain cosmic consciousness. This influence also enables the to delve into and solve mysteries.

Tenth House: They are experts at bringing about financial growth in business, and are best when working with their creative, investigative minds. They organize their jobs behind the scenes, so it looks as if they do things effortlessly. Their conservatism isn't apparent for they appear to be loose and free.

Eleventh House: They have few friends they trust and even then do not confide everything to them. Ever curious, they want to know what lies behind what people say. They are constantly aware, and want to know all about everyone else, but want few, if any, to know their secrets.

Twelfth House: Even though they may be emotional about their sex life, they may hide their sensitive and feeling nature, showing the world a more extroverted image. There are karmic conditions connected with sex, and the death of someone close will bring about a drastic change.

Scorpio-Cancer, Third Decanate, 20-30⁰, Spiritual

Scorpio-Cancer Ascendant
First House: Most see these people as strong, confident, and enduring. The emotional nature is often released through domestic affairs or religious affiliations, and the religious nature directed by a strong emotional pull. They have hypnotic personalities that can be used to give others strength and emotional healing.

Second House: These people are happy when their houses or places of business are more homey. Their offices may even be located in their places of residence. They know what people want and draw others into their orbit like magnets. As a result, they easily add to their own resources by giving them what they want.

Third House: Emotional attachment can lead them to study a subject when reason or logic cannot. They enjoy entertaining at home, but do not necessarily make a habit of it. Even though they do not readily join community organizations, they will work hard if it is a good cause.

Fourth House: If there is anything wrong on the domestic scene, these people hide it. They put up a good front so that others will think all is fine. This influence can indicate karmic conditions within the family. They keep deeper emotions to themselves, and even though they do not show it, they need to be loved and cared for.

Fifth House: These people are intense in their attachment to children, partly in reaction to a childhood memory that cannot be overcome. They crave extra measures of love that they seem to absorb like water, and they also can have secret love affairs or a child no one knows about.

Sixth House: Work is a part of life, and these people get the facts and use them well in fulfilling their job duties. They may not be emotional but they know how to play on the emotions of employees and employers in order to increase job benefits, whether financial or cooperative.

Seventh House: These people have deep, possessive feelings, and may keep secrets from their partners or associates. They are loyal, protective, sympathetic, and tenacious, and although they may encounter changes within relationships, they remain loyal and marriage endures. But they suffer greatly if things go wrong, and may have a tendency smother those they love.

Eighth House: Although deeply sensuous, these people never talk about their sexual intimacies. For them, sex is emotionally laden as well as personal and private. Because they don't discuss their problems with anyone, they can develop ulcers or other health problems, especially if something is not right with a relationship.

Ninth House: They have strong mental powers, and meditation can bring new insights and philosophies. A tendency to be fixed and emotional in attitude may be a stumbling block in their search for the truth. They need to learn to be more flexible so they can receive the full intuitive value of this position.

Tenth House: These people produce results, and they labor hard to do an excellent job. They will observe the results, and if are not to their liking, they will re-do the job. The people they work with are like second families to them. These are the people with whom everyone unburdens their problems.

Eleventh House: These people are loyal friends, and even though they seem cold at times, they are soft and gentle to their partners, whether in marriage or friendship. Emotions deepen as time passes. They may mother others or attract partners who will mother them.

Twelfth House: These people don't always like their emotional attitude about sex, so they unconsciously build up complexes they must eventually transcend. They try to keep this part of their nature under cover, and must learn to bring sex out of hiding and into its proper regenerative role in love.

Sagittarius-Sagittarius, First Decanate, 0-10°, Physical

Sagittarius-Sagittarius Ascendant
First House: These people are abstract thinkers, and the initial projection into physical activity is through adventure in sports, fun, and travel. They develop great pride in their own ideas and have the ability to inspire others, but must learn to balance the adventurous spirit with teaching others abstract ideas.

Second House: They think in terms of long-range income, looking ahead, and as a result increase income in more than one way. Generous, they spend a great deal of their income, but somehow always make more. Intuition is strong for improving their resources as a representation of their life work or destiny.

Third House: Extroverts who know how to talk with people, they see the broad view and like moving about and taking adventurous trips. They know how to respond and thus can easily cultivate friends and contacts. Well-liked, they are often sought-after guests on the social scene.

Fourth House: These people always do right by the family, and like to invite people to the home to discuss philosophical subjects and the latest developments. Some hold classes in the home, but they always want a bigger and better one. Some have two homes. Their high morals are beyond question.

Fifth House: Usually enthusiastic and optimistic, they tend to initiate too many ideas themselves and need to let loved ones do this at times. They tend to put loved ones on a pedestal, and have an innate ability to inspire children, young people, and romantic interests. But they need to bring their emotions out into the open, good or bad.

Sixth House: They prefer larger jobs with brighter futures or that provide more satisfaction, and can be excellent workers if the job allows them to travel physically or mentally. For example, some teach or work in the travel industry. Serving others as a philosophy of life takes priority.

Seventh House: These people have original and independent views on marriage, and often marry friends, believing that companionship is most important. They may travel with the partner or on behalf of the partner. Integrity, honesty, and loyalty are important even though at times they do not want to be held too tightly.

Eighth House: These people have strict sexual codes, and conservative ideas. They also have the instinct for managing large sums of money and for giving financial advice. In the area of finance their view is big-picture. Most attract mates who have much money or the potential to gain it.

Ninth House: These people can predict the future because of their keen insight. They size up situations or ideas, see how they will progress, and carry them to conclusion. Intuition is strong, and they are future-oriented optimists who embrace new levels of growth and understanding.

Tenth House: These visionaries are lucky in their career choice and in setting goals. They are best in a traveling job where they can use their restless nature creatively rather than in a non-productive way. They are also good counselors. Their ideas are expansive, and these people are bound to advance.

Eleventh House: Generous and genial with their many friends, they are fair to all, regardless of how close or how remote they may be. These people are not apt to be solicitous of one over the other. They are broad-minded and can accept differences of opinion among their friends.

Twelfth House: Sagittarians with this position may be critical about religion but will keep ideas to themselves. Even so, their attitudes will seem practical to others. Some work hard for religious groups or in higher education, and they are often mentally way ahead of their associates.

Sagittarius-Aries, Second Decanate, 10-20°, Mental

Sagittarius-Aries Ascendant

First House: This influence gives a tendency for excessive enthusiasm; they start with a burst of energy and then lose interest. It gives a tremendous sense of humor. When the energy is used to pioneer trends and ideas, it is invaluable. The same is true of creative endeavors of an artistic nature.

Second House: Very generous with resources, these people know that the more they give, the more they get. They have the mental drive to give and serve others, and can make money from pioneering new and different ideas in writing, publishing, teaching, journalism, etc.

Third House: These people spread news around the neighborhood, and are the first to be aware of situations. This may or may not sit well with the partner, but these people enjoy sharing news because of their natural curiosity. The lesser self will spread gossip, while the higher self will teach others.

Fourth House: Even though they are the leaders of groups that meet in the home, they are quite secretive about their own beliefs. They put on airs in order to appear to be very religious or moral, but often there is a skeleton in the closet. However, they are concerned with the betterment of others.

Fifth House: These people believe their lives are destined for something special and that they are guided by a larger force. They can be show-offs. They will gamble whatever they have for love or for their religious philosophies, and are fearless in affairs of the heart or where children are concerned.

Sixth House: Never underestimate their capacity to plan for the future and to reach their goals. It is a sure-fire combination for success. They may appear shy but when it comes to work that leads to further advancement, they are go-getters and pioneers. They know what they want and will not settle for less.

Seventh House: The partner must share their desire to be on the go, and they also like friends and partners who enlarge upon or follow up their ideas. They also need broad-minded partners who understand their continual bursts of enthusiasm and short-lived efforts with constructive projects.

Eighth House: Behind everything they is a hidden motive. These people are driven to follow moral codes, but also need to prove how fearless they can be (which can conflict at times with other things in their lives). They have a deep faith even though they tend to be conventional in their approach.

Ninth House: These people pioneer new trends and have the capacity to see how these innovations will work out in the future. They set things in motion using great insight for growth, and are even better at this as they age and become more open to higher cosmic consciousness.

Tenth House: These people have a certain amount of luck and, by exerting much energy along with it, they succeed and acquire quite a bit of money. However, they spend it fast. They are out in the open with beliefs and want faith to inspire others to do something special.

Eleventh House: They have many friends and could be leaders in groups with advanced ideas, communicating these ideas to other groups. These people have a need to inform others and to incite them to activity, and are interested in enlarging humanity's awareness. If they can do this, they feel fulfilled.

Twelfth House: These people have a subconscious drive for intellectual superiority, and want to understand all of the hidden laws of nature. They may hide their desire for leadership for a while, but faith in themselves, motivated by strong family energy, finally pushes them out into the open with an irresistible force.

Sagittarius-Leo, Third Decanate, 20-30°, Spiritual

Sagittarius-Leo Ascendant

First House: This gives awareness of divine consciousness, and these people are involved as teachers or leaders, possibly of religion. They are natural, charming promoters and therefore can be overly enthusiastic. However, they are fun-loving and have great expectations for all.

Second House: These people want to make money and a name for themselves. Goal-oriented, this gives great talent for planning the future. While they tend to spend money freely, they always have sufficient funds. It is best if they are in business for themselves where they can be creative in many ways.

Third House: These people like long trips for fun and education. They take pictures and show them to friends, and enjoy talking about their many adventures. They treat those they entertain like royalty; however, they do prefer to socialize with people who are important or intellectual.

Fourth House: These people enjoy privacy in the home and always do what is right for the family. They fail most of the time to receive the recognition they deserve. The tendency is to work behind the scenes for the person on the throne, which can result in martyrdom or self-sacrifice.

Fifth House: These people are capable of building high ideals in those they touch with love. They are generous, extravagant, and like to impress others, but they need to take care not to overdo giving, especially with loved ones. They can be egotistical and arrogant, and may put loved ones on a pedestal.

Sixth House: These people work because they believe they are doing something important and because they want to accumulate beautiful possessions. They love artistic creations and crave to have them in the home. They are the story-tellers at work for they love fun and games.

Seventh House: Even after they are married they roam freely because they love to communicate and entertain the people around them. Their need for self-expression supersedes everything else. They sometimes have too many interests, so it is difficult for them to narrow their focus. Whenever pushed, they want to break free.

Eighth House: These people love to entertain lovers at home in a lavish way. Sexual communion (and communion is exactly what it is to them) must have eye-pleasing surroundings. They also have a talent for large-scale business, and can be especially lucky if they invest in real estate or entertainment.

Ninth House: A broad, optimistic outlook is behind their belief in love and its ability to give strength and cheerfulness. They crave applause and can dramatize enthusiasm for religious reform, thereby influencing others, and will support legal action that involves the betterment of children or of the arts.

Tenth House: These people have big ideas but their hearts must be in their careers or they don't do well. They also need to have strong leadership roles. Charming, they have the know-how to attract people because they know just what to say. They think big and usually get big results.

Eleventh House: These people do things in a big way for friends. They may be loose and free, enjoying comradery with friends, but these people can attract partners who will dominate them. Friends can live anywhere, and they will travel as necessary to maintain these relationships.

Twelfth House: Some are anonymous donors to religious and other worthwhile causes. They can be very spiritual or not, but when they give of themselves they experience spiritual expansion. However, they never talk about the partner's financial situation or marital problems.

Capricorn-Capricorn, First Decanate, 0-10°, Physical

Capricorn-Capricorn Ascendant
First House: These people are born serious and should watch a tendency to become too disciplined. The result can be calcium deposits in their joints as they age. They will work very hard and will sacrifice much for ambition as they want to be seen as authorities in their field, which may mean more than financial success.

Second House: They cautiously guard finances because security means a lot to them. The Sagittarius Ascendant may give the urge to gamble, but it is doubtful they will risk money and investments. They gamble in other ways that might boost financial security.

Third House: These people do not like small talk, but they need to relax when communicating with others and learn to laugh. They may not be interested in education when they are young, but mental talents grow and expand as they age. They strive to gain acceptance and prestige, and desire to appear wise.

Fourth House: They desire to be accepted by the public even in a limited way. Conservative with family, they are often strong disciplinarians. They don't like to change and hate to move, and want a strong, sturdy home. The desire to acquire possessions is strong, which can present problems in home life.

Fifth House: They need to learn to relax in affairs of the heart as rigidity can hinder love and make them too austere in their relationship with children, young people, and romantic lovers. They have a strong sense of duty and responsibility to the people they love and tend to be protective of them.

Sixth House: They feel a strong sense of duty toward work and are dependable. These people are the ones to call for difficult jobs because they work long hours. They worry about their health, which can lead to hypochondria. Competence and dedication usually result in financial success.

Seventh House: The marriage partner may be older or serious, and these people will endure an unhappy marriage out of loyalty. However, if Saturn is afflicted, the marriage may fail no matter how hard they try. They accept responsibilities connected with marriage that others do not.

Eighth House: They need to learn that sex cannot be organized or treated with a cold mental outlook. They should learn to be more extemporaneous with sex and to enjoy it more. They can be overly concerned and responsible for the partner's finances, which can cause trouble.

Ninth House: Beliefs must be backed by logical evidence, but they go along with authorities in dealing with society's laws. They do not like to travel unless the trip is necessary and practical, and they are not apt to stray too far from the religious beliefs of their forebears.

Tenth House: They are organized with everything and everyone. Because they know they will not get something for nothing, they are willing to work for it. They will avoid trouble if they can, for they do not want to stain their reputation. They keep climbing until they get to the top.

Eleventh House: These people keep the friendships they make, and they may prefer older or more serious-minded friends. They do not like a lot of people around them, so they do not have many friends. They are selective about those with whom they share confidences.

Twelfth House: They are friendly, worldly, liberal, and the forerunners of human progress, but they live solitary lives. They secretly lack confidence and need to learn to accept themselves first before they can fully help others. They sometimes have deep inner sorrows.

Capricorn-Taurus, Second Decanate, 10-20°, Mental

Capricorn-Taurus Ascendant

First House: Whatever they do must serve a useful purpose. They are conservative but have a natural flair for using creative energy, which is usually profitable. They are ambitious and use mental energy to gain prestige and money, but they need to learn to relax and have fun merely for fun's sake. Although not the most expressive lover, they are protective and loyal.

Second House: These people are very serious about work and finances. They approach the career in ways to make as much money as possible, which is the whole reason for the career as far as they're concerned. They will not spend on junk food, and gifts that have no value go into the garbage.

Third House: Serious in thought and controlled in communication, these people respond to beauty and affection. They seem more flexible than they really are, and although few reach their inner circle, they are loyal to those who do. Whatever they do seems to turn into money, even if it doesn't start out that way.

Fourth House: These people take pride in an organized, beautiful home, preferably one owned by them with enough land for gardening and enjoying nature. They are materialistic and know how to acquire resources, and enjoy entertaining in order to showcase their achievements.

Fifth House: In love these people are serious, responsible, loyal, and sensuous, and they can be possessive. For fun they enjoy social events, bazaars, and carnivals. They are disciplinarians with their children and expect them to earn their own spending money.

Sixth House: These people work hard because they feel it is their duty and because they enjoy status and the power that comes with authority. Once they attain power they do not easily give it up. They need to learn to let others help them, for they tend to do everything themselves.

Seventh House: These people may be financially conservative with a partner, only to be big spenders with friends. The partner needs to understand that friends are a basic need and a rich resource. Loyal and devoted in friendship and marriage, they need a partner who's also a friend.

Eighth House: They can be unsentimental yet very sensuous in love. These people make good financiers of other people's money and usually have a knack for any kind of investment. They are uneasy about their own financial needs so they usually have more than one source of income.

Ninth House: While they are pleasant, they incline to be conservative with their spiritual lives. In the area of philosophical thought and ideas they learn to relate to these ideas through experience. Little has meaning for them until they have lived it or seen it work.

Tenth House: These people rise in their careers simply because they want to be first and do not like to take orders. They are able to pioneer new territory with great income potential, and purchase things that will increase in value. Energy goes into making money, and they do nothing that will be a detriment to their career.

Eleventh House: These people have few intimate friends. While they may seem free and flexible to casual acquaintances, true and tested friends know how stubborn they can be. Friends will appeal to them through their poetic sense of beauty (Pisces Ascendant).

Twelfth House: These people may be far ahead of the times with some of their ideas, but the nature is more fixed and conservative than is apparent. Because of this, their ideas may not get too far off the ground, or they may become too practical and materialistic. It depends upon where Uranus and Saturn are in the chart

Capricorn-Virgo, Third Decanate, 20-30°, Spiritual

Capricorn- Virgo Ascendant
First House: Health is not the best when young, but they grow stronger with age. Practical and careful (fussy at times), they will sacrifice physical comfort for ambition. Success comes in part through following the rules. This decanate is more flexible than the other Capricorn decanates.

Second House: These people carefully guard possessions, monitor spending, and are ambitious to acquire great wealth. They prefer working for large companies, feeling it is financially safer and more beneficial. There is also a greater opportunity to advance in a larger organization.

Third House: They are the odd ones in the family. Because they are not always understood, they are uncommunicative until they move away from home. Interested in serious subjects, they are not good at small talk. What they enjoy is listening to others talk about themselves.

Fourth House: These people are secretly critical, and even though they may not voice their criticism, it can affect their health. Strong drives to keep the household organized can sap their energy and make them feel insecure. They worry about little details while neglecting the big ones.

Fifth House: These people are seekers of perfection, so they are apt to be critical of their loved ones. Turned to the positive, they can feel great pride in unselfishly serving loved ones. All work and no play makes them lose spontaneity, and they can be too structured even in fun and games. Fun many times turns into work.

Sixth House: They are efficient workers but may work so hard that their health can suffer. These people worry a great deal about finances, and save on little things so they can buy the big things. They feel a deep responsibility to their work and are perfectionists who can work themselves into a nervous frazzle.

Seventh House: These people attract ambitious partners. Although they can be sentimental, the tendency toward criticism can restrict emotional expression. They may attract mates who will want to be protected and cared for, ones who either have health problems or are hypochondriacs.

Eighth House: If you don't know them well, they appear to be carefree, but for the sake of their health they need a place of peace and quiet. They may be unsentimental and discriminating in their sex life, but they make good detectives or researchers.

Ninth House: They are too stiff in their self-expression and tend to follow the dictates of authority in religion and social law. These people are not gamblers where religious views are concerned. They are very discriminating and want a sure thing in ideas and affections.

Tenth House: This gives ambition, hard work, organizational ability, and a talent for putting up with petty details if it advances their aims. However, they can end up nervous and irritated but will come out fine if left alone. They know how to take care of themselves. Some take five-minute catnaps.

Eleventh House: Friendships are few but solid and good. They do a lot for friends even though they may be a bit critical of them at times. They usually give in to what the majority of the group wants and then cater to the group.

Twelfth House: They have brilliant ideas and can uncover many secrets. These people secretly feel criticism even if not actually voiced by anyone, which can hinder brilliant ideas coming out in the open. They can block their own progress by picking others apart. If used positively, they work hard in the service of humanity.

Aquarius-Aquarius, First Decanate, 0-10°, Physical

Aquarius-Aquarius Ascendant
First House: Their creativity is unconventional and original. They are eager to present new ideas regarding the right of individual self-expression, and they stand out in a crowd as different and unique, either in looks or how they dress. They are ahead of the times and are considered original and creative or erratic and radical.

Second House: They need and earn money because they want to be free, and they associate financial resources with freedom. Otherwise, they are not affected too much by financial considerations. Income may fluctuate, but somehow they always have money. Their financial philosophy is usually ahead of the times.

Third House: Continually interested in new concepts, experiences, and ideas, in many cases they are self-made people. They are the ones who break the mold, and are extremely friendly and talk with everyone. To them, every neighbor is a brother or sister.

Fourth House: This gives sudden changes in the home life, and is conducive to unconventional attitudes about the domestic scene. They want to be free from being too committed to a home or family. These people easily renew themselves and can break clean of anything with ease and start over again.

Fifth House: They believe in love affairs in or out of the marriage bond, and are impatient with facades, believing in the individual need to follow real love. Their children may be out of the ordinary, or unusual conditions may result from or with children.

Sixth House: When they work, they want to do things their way, and can get into trouble on the job because of this. They need jobs where they can put into practice their special and original ideas, and may do well with self-employment. This position also indicates inner tension or poor circulation.

Seventh House: The marriage relationship is always subject to changing conditions and is extraordinary in some way. There will be unusual experiences with it, such as differences in age, race, religion, etc. They attract mates who are very independent or who are friends. Open enemies become friends.

Eighth House: They believe in sexual freedom, and are have progressive views, taking a stand when others do not. They are inclined to accept astrology and metaphysical studies, and have insatiable thirst for universal law. Constant curiosity puts them in front in this type of study.

Ninth House: They believe religion should keep up with the times, and usually also have advanced ideas about education. Even though they have liberal views, they usually express them in a very reasonable manner so that everyone can understand.

Tenth House: They need to be their own boss, in a career where they can be independent, or in a business that produces avant-garde items. Their careers follow an erratic pattern, and they make friends among coworkers. Aviation or electronics may appeal to them. Their jobs should benefit humanity in some way.

Eleventh House: They will attract friends who are as original and individualistic as they are. They become part of groups bent upon changing the world. Their groups of friends believe in the concept that all men are equal, and they do not like dull companions and have little tolerance for them.

Twelfth House: They may be great psychics, but may not share their experiences. If they can finally break their silence and come through, these people can be among the greatest voices of a higher consciousness in revealing cosmic truths. They need to break free and help people with their talents.

Aquarius-Gemini, Second Decanate, 10-20°, Mental

Aquarius-Gemini Ascendant

First House: They are friendly, light and easy, and others feel as though they have known these people for a long time. Their friendliness remains detached, however, in part because they need to be free and on the move. They express themselves well and are the catalysts who stir the minds of others.

Second House: They usually have a variety of ways to earn income, and have original ideas to increase productivity for profit. Although they want to get ahead and can have high earnings, money does not control them. They know just how different to make things in order to have wide appeal.

Third House: Somehow original ideas and a great creative mind operate with and/or in connection with friends or partners. They work best as a team, are intent upon educating others in a most original manner. This is perfect for a training team, especially if the partner has an Aquarius-Gemini Sun or a Gemini-Aquarius Sun.

Fourth House: These people are not what they seem to be. Fate seems to split them from family, and some have more than one home. They rejuvenate and renew themselves through discussion and expression in order to break free from emotional or mental restrictions caused by the family or domestic affairs.

Fifth House: When it comes to romance, they live the intensity more in their heads than in actual association. They engage in unconventional love affairs that remain rather cool and detached. If a romantic situation gets too heavy, they institute sudden breaks. They prefer attachments where they can pursue abstract theories.

Sixth House: They work best when they remain impersonal in coworker relationships. They communicate easily with them, but mostly daily communication is about the job or casual subjects. They may have two jobs at once, and are best when moving about communicating with all types of people.

Seventh House: A partnership will have a multitude of friends that either augments the relationship or causes friction. If they have a mate as individualistic and enthused about a number of things as they are, they will work together as a team. If they are friends as well as partners, it will work beautifully.

Eighth House: They have original ideas about sex, and also accept those of others. They are curious and inquisitive, and much of the label they get about being sexy hides a mind that wants to learn more of the real truth behind birth and death and what it means metaphysically.

Ninth House: These people can be very persuasive and make others believe almost anything. They like to think they know something about everything, and they probably do. These people can identify not only with the higher mind but with conscious understanding of it, and thus communicate with a wide variety of people.

Tenth House: These people benefit from service careers, and there is a dual aspect to the career. There may operate in two places, and use originality and cleverness to make money, acquiring a large amount. Any career that involves a lot of talking with people is beneficial.

Eleventh House: This gives two distinct groups of friends, with one group separate from the other. They understand each friend individually, and dislike boring people. There are many short trips with friends, and brothers and sisters are also friends.

Twelfth House: They are psychic, and there is no field of the occult in which they will not experiment. Somehow they often feel as if they are not in the right environment or that they are not on the right planet or right level. They fight to be free, but continually feel locked in.

Aquarius-Libra, Third Decanate, 20-30°, Spiritual

Aquarius-Libra Ascendant

First House: They seek truth and fight hard for equality, remaining independent and free even though they are very friendly and exceptionally understanding and kind. They identify with each but still maintain very strong originality. Their curiosity to acquire more and more knowledge is insatiable.

Second House: They can be impersonal about money and do not let it control them. Yet, if someone is unfair about their wages, they surely will argue. They can excel financially through sales or dealing with large numbers of people. Their sense of fairness and humanitarianism brings success.

Third House: These people have original ideas and delight in lively discussion. They are interested in people, everyone from neighbors to others around the world, and want everyone to be heard who wants to be heard. It is easy for them to bring different friends and groups together who have varying opinions.

Fourth House: Home conditions may be more unconventional than average, or there may be upsetting domestic situations. The marriage partnership may involve a secret alliance, or there may be something one keeps from the other because he or she will not understand.

Fifth House: This decanate of Aquarius operates more from a need for pure spiritual love, but a love that is different. One of the partners is original and ingenious. The need to associate through a unique partner is great, as is the need for creative self-expression through relationships.

Sixth House: They can be original and ingenious, and too independent, but charm lets them get by with it. They are the diplomats in a group of employees, and are sociable and work easily in groups. These people work because they like to spend money on objects of quality and fine workmanship.

Seventh House: Independence and rebellion could be issues regarding a partner because of a tendency to be too individualistic. However, with the Libra influence these people will want to preserve peace. Both people should try hard not to dominate the other; then it will work.

Eighth House: They may be original and crave freedom in sex, but deep in the roots of their beings they need a partner and a beautiful home. They instinctively know the real beauty and rejuvenating power of sex. Even with all of their beliefs in sexual freedom, they are not apt to use it as license for promiscuity.

Ninth House: These people are scientific and unorthodox in religion and philosophy, but when love enters the picture, they may defer a little of their independent originality to the mate's ideas. They are sociable and want to be accepted, so this can modify their liberal philosophies.

Tenth House: They are cooperative and want to help people in their careers. They are the arbitrators who believe in unions and fair trade. Even though they have a tendency to do their own thing, they accept the ideas of others in a diplomatic fashion acceptable to all concerned.

Eleventh House: They need both a partner and friends to share their lives, people with whom they can pursue their intellectual curiosity. These people do a lot of socializing because they are friendly and need people around them. This gives great spiritual understanding of others.

Twelfth House: Their unconventional nature and conditions in marriages remain under wraps, and there may be karmic conditions with friends in relation to the marriage partner. They can be very objective concerning the study of occult laws, and when they need to regenerate, they will go off alone.

Pisces-Pisces, First Decanate, 0-10°, Physical

Pisces-Pisces Ascendant
First House: These people have vivid imaginations and can be very impressionable. This gives a psychic talent that mayor may not be fully realized, and they don't always know exactly who they are and where they are going. At best, they should become involved in a cause for humanity, and avoid escapism.

Second House: These people are not good with money and should never invest in risky enterprises. But they're also extremely generous even if they have to do without themselves. Yet somehow the money they need eventually does arrive even if it's always tomorrow.

Third House: They are dreamers. However, their vivid imagination can be very artistic and fulfill a positive mode of self-expression that's necessary for them. They can be psychic. Sometimes, however, they can become lost in self-pity, which needs to be controlled in order to make the most of this position.

Fourth House: The domestic situation may calls for great sacrifice, and there is a feeling of uncertainty in domestic affairs or with a parent. A secret may be part of the family heritage. At its best, this influence can enhance compassion and understanding in caring for others.

Fifth House: Their love experiences are out of the ordinary, and they are self-sacrificing and idealistic. It may give a gifted child, an unusual child, or a highly spiritual one. They are poetic in self-expression, and words flow in beautiful form. They may be musical in the sense of composition.

Sixth House: When these people are ill, it can be difficult to diagnose the cause. They do not function at their best on jobs where details need attention. But if they believe in a cause they can sacrifice much time, work, and effort. However, they must focus on an ideal in order to be most productive.

Seventh House: They may be too idealistic for marriage, and need to be cautious about aligning themselves with people because they feel sorry for them. However, they can attract soul mates or relationships with great spiritual affinity. A partner could have a drinking problem. They need to learn to be more tolerant of partners.

Eighth House: When they have problems with sex, they do not know exactly why. They can be too idealistic concerning sexual performance, as well as sacrificial. This influence is not good for business affairs because financial matters are not straightforward. Others can cheat them and hide financial facts.

Ninth House: This may give spiritualistic tendencies with regard to religion. It gives faith in unseen forces, and the belief that people can advance to a higher spiritual love for others. Some are in touch with the higher intelligence of the universe and do not embrace orthodox religion.

Tenth House: With regard to the career they should have all the cards on the table from the start in order to avoid deception in the future. They may present an image to the public that is the furthest thing from the reality of what they are. Somehow what they do, or the motive behind it, doesn't come across to people.

Eleventh House: Friends will either be inspiring and spiritual or rather unreliable, and people with this influence can be gullible, idealistic, and sacrificing where friends are concerned. At best they can give unselfishly of their time and effort to humanitarian causes.

Twelfth House: These people may have psychosomatic illnesses, and suffer from a deep inner loneliness. Sensitivity often comes from the subconscious, from hidden memories and experiences, and they can do well in service to others who are ill, physically, emotionally, or mentally.

Pisces-Cancer, Second Decanate, 10-20°, Mental

Pisces-Cancer Ascendant
First House: These people have a need to be nurtured and a need for self-sacrifice. They know some traits are instinctive, but above and beyond that their goals remain hidden from themselves. They are driven to creative work with or because of the people they love.

Second House: These people can make money because they sense what the public wants. But they may spend their money on dreams and bubbles. If this is carried to the fullest, with Cancer on the sixth house, working conditions may be a second home and coworkers a second family.

Third House: These people are aware of hidden influences within the environment, or hidden meanings behind what people say. They seek marriage partners with whom they can talk about these subtle feelings and those who share an awareness of nature. They sense things others miss.

Fourth House: Willing to make great sacrifices for the family, they seem unable to forget the past, and are driven to discover the mysteries of their life and death and the whys of birth, past lives, and other esoteric wisdom. They seek a deeper meaning and identity.

Fifth House: These people get what they desire because their timing is excellent and they know instinctively what they must sacrifice for love and creativity. They project sentimental feelings in love, which gives them the impetus to study higher truths.

Sixth House: Although they rarely work harder than anyone else, their instincts for knowing what people want enhance their options for success and high earnings. But coworkers can hurt their feelings, causing them to make mountains out of molehills.

Seventh House: They need sympathetic friends and marriage partners, and can make great sacrifices for people they love. These are the people who decline marriage in order to take care of a parent or to pursue a great and noble cause.

Eighth House: They rejuvenate themselves with time alone in a special place at home where the atmosphere is exactly right to revitalize them. They can sublimate passion and sex drive through work of love for mankind. Vacations near the sea or sailing rejuvenate them greatly.

Ninth House: They ultimately need to know the reason for existence on earth. The greatest motivation to studying higher truths, religion, and philosophy comes from subconscious drives, and they are innately aware that they have much instinctive knowledge. They deeply understand spiritual love, and they are psychic.

Tenth House: These people know instinctively how the public will respond, and they gravitate to careers that make the most of this. However, they often do not know what they themselves want. Communication is a must in a job, and some are happiest with two jobs, especially in the service industry.

Eleventh House: These people have real sympathy for friends and will go the extra mile to spend time with them and help with their problems. The attitude is: "My home is my friends' home. If you are a friend, you are welcome." Emotional ties with friends are especially strong.

Twelfth House: These people have great self-pride, and if home life is good, they are happy and outgoing. However, domestic and family problems cause them to suffer in silence and martyrdom. They will sacrifice a great deal for home and family comfort.

Pisces-Scorpio, Third Decanate, 20-30°, Spiritual

Pisces-Scorpio Ascendant
First House: Behind a compassionate, understanding approach is a strong individual with much self-assurance. There is a willingness to sacrifice physical comforts in order to study the higher-realm subject, or some simply ignore physical necessities. Mental and spiritual values are especially of interest.

Second House: Once committed to a job, they will stand by it or die in the attempt. They never seem to have enough money, for their outgo is most of the time greater than their income. If they do not worry about it, it usually takes care of itself. More important is that they use creativity in efforts of the mind and natural inventiveness.

Third House: Secretive about their own affairs, they want to know the hidden factors behind what other people say and do. They are loyal and devoted to friends and neighbors, and expect the same from others. There may be secret friends and alliances.

Fourth House: These people like to move about, but there is really no place like home. They are willing to sacrifice much for family, but tend to be secretive about what goes on in the home. There is a deep desire within them to unravel the real reason for sex, besides procreation. They have strong leanings toward genetic research.

Fifth House: These people have secret love affairs and may be turned off by conventional relationships. Because they have strong sexual and emotional idealism, their love affairs may be unhappy. However, when they finally find the ideal, they are magnificent and can endure anything, rising to true spiritual love.

Sixth House: They do not like physical labor, and instead manipulate others to do the work. They rarely reveal how much money they make. Getting the best of their talents requires work where they can cater to people who are ill, old, or suffering, and they excel in work where people are more or less helpless.

Seventh House: Capable of great sacrifices for their partners, including financial ones, they hide their true relationship from the world. They need a partner's shoulder to cry on when necessary, as well as one who is emotionally and mentally supportive.

Eighth House: They rejuvenate themselves through an innate love for humanity, and have strong feelings about inheritance—not just money but also family (pride) heritage. Life gives them experiences for humility in order to be reborn into greater spiritual love and a sense of equality and oneness with all.

Ninth House: Even though they are psychic and can understand the truth of the universe, they never lose their own identities in doing so. The more evolved attain cosmic consciousness. They can uncover secrets, and are creative and artistic, leaning heavily on the mysteries of love, where they can be possessive.

Tenth House: They are best at careers where they use their creative and investigative minds. Although they like job variability, or are indecisive as to what they want to do, they will stand by a commitment until it is finished. They need to know their work is of service to others.

Eleventh House: These people have great sympathy for their friends and are hurt if others don't sympathize with them. There is an inclination to work hard and to acquire a great deal of money doing it, which is often passed on to favorite charities. They can be possessive and jealous.

Twelfth House: These people have deep feelings and intense sexual passion. They often are community leaders who present an image far different from their personal one. Extremely realistic about life, they are purposeful in all they do, directing their energy into ambitions.

Chapter 5

Degree Meanings

When dealing with individual degrees you must consider the sign and its natural inclinations; the decanate (physical, mental or spiritual, and the co-ruler); and the nature of the degree number vibration.

For example, with Aries, first decanate, all degrees of this decanate would have the Aries-Aries nature and a physical vibration. Numbers 1 through 10 are described as follows:

1. Self-initiative and self-reliance.
2. Cooperation with another. Go after it. You make the effort.
3. Expression of ideas and cheerfulness.
4. Skillfully putting practical things together that work. Routine!
5. Dealing with variety or change. Promoting something.
6. Responsibility for someone or something other than self.
7. Learning mastery and perfection.
8. Making others aware of the mastery and capitalizing upon it.
9. Being generous and loveable. The big brother or sister type.
10. The completion of one dimension and the arrival at another. The end and the beginning. Awareness of cosmic help.

The degrees 11-20 are the mental decanate. As an example, Aries-Leo would be described as having an Aries-Leo nature with mental influences. Take the influence already described above and correspond it with 11-20.

The degrees 21-30 have a spiritual influence. All numbers in this decanate then respond to Aries-Sagittarius, and the same influence as 1-10. But remember, it is a higher vibration and dimension.

It is a question of dimensional differences, like plateaus. Just take the influence as stated in 1₵10 and add either the mental influence or the spiritual, depending upon the decanate. The same pattern is true of all of the signs and their degrees. Just individualize them, remembering the rules.

Masculine/Feminine

Next we divide the 30-degree sign into two 15-degree halves, of which one is positive (masculine) and one is negative (feminine). A person born within the first 15 degrees of Aries responds to a masculine, positive vibration; the last 15 degrees is feminine and negative. The masculine half of each sign is co-ruled by the Sun and therefore projective. The feminine half is co-ruled by the Moon and receptive.

The following interpretations are according to the masculine and feminine influence of the divided 30-degree signs (15 degrees each). It is primarily interpreted as a positive or negative influence of the sign traits, but house position and aspects will modify this to a greater or lesser degree.

Aries, 0-15°, Masculine, Positive, Electric

The first half of Aries gives courage and the ability to act upon that courage. These people are enterprising with a good use of dynamic ideas.

Aries, 16-30°, Feminine, Negative, Magnetic

This half of Aries is more arrogant, much more inclined to be impulsive and combative.

Taurus, 0-15°, Feminine, Negative, Magnetic

This half of Taurus is more stubborn, more materialistic. There is also a tendency to be self-indulgent.

Taurus, 16-30°, Masculine, Positive, Electric

This portion is more reliable. They are patient, enduring, and determined.

Gemini, 0-15°, Masculine, Positive, Electric

There is an alertness, and they are inquisitive and expressive.

Gemini, 16-30°, Feminine, Negative, Magnetic

This feminine half may make the natives more shallow because they try to cover too much ground for variety. They also need to learn to listen to others talk.

Cancer, 0-15°, Feminine, Negative, Magnetic

This indicates excessive sensitivity or touchiness, and there may be a clannish tendency. Receptivity to psychic impressions is also strong.

Cancer, 16-30°, Masculine, Positive, Electric

These people are home-loving, with a great interest in the family. They are also constructive and talented in anything domestic, from repairs to decorating and sewing.

Leo, 0-15°, Masculine, Positive, Electric

A great virtue is being loving and affectionate, and they are loyal and faithful to the core. This is the actor, whether on stage or in everyday life.

Leo, 16-30°, Feminine, Negative, Magnetic

This half of the sign may have a show-off tendency, but it may not be an outward expression of acting as in the masculine half of the sign. It may instead show up as egotism and a domineering, commanding attitude.

Virgo, 0-15°, Feminine, Negative, Magnetic

A critical and fussy demeanor comes through with this position. It also gives worry over health matters.

Virgo, 16-30°, Masculine, Positive, Electric

These people are thorough and methodical with a tendency toward neatness. They are excellent in their service to the ill.

Libra, 0-15°, Masculine, Positive, Electric

These people are fair and exceptionally gracious. They are refined in manner, and have a talent for the arts.

Libra, 16-30°, Feminine, Negative, Magnetic

These people are indecisive with a tendency for dependence. Perhaps another trait of theirs is peace at any price—to the extent of giving in too easily.

Scorpio, 0-15°, Feminine, Negative, Magnetic

There is jealousy, and an inclination to be secretive, suspicious, and vengeful. However, there is also strong magnetic power with the opposite sex.

Scorpio, 16-30°, Masculine, Positive, Electric

These people are heroic and determined, with great fortitude. It also gives a strong healing quality, for they exude strength and rejuvenating energy.

Sagittarius, 0-15°, Masculine, Positive, Electric

They are optimistic, philosophical, and generous. There is also a tendency for joviality, and they see the big view.

Sagittarius, 16-30°, Feminine, Negative, Magnetic

These people are restless, sometimes foolhardy and freedom-loving. They also may gamble, perhaps overdoing it.

Capricorn, 0-15°, Feminine, Negative, Magnetic

These people are patronizing, autocratic, and overly thrifty. Being overly cautious prevents them from seizing good opportunities, and they also need to be aware of a tendency for melancholia.

Capricorn, 16-30°, Masculine, Positive, Electric

These people are ambitious and overly conscious of their duties and responsibilities. Many seek status among their peers, and steady, determined effort ensures success.

Aquarius, 0-15°, Masculine, Positive, Electric

These people are friendly, mentally original, and very progressive. They are platonic and helpful, but can easily walk away from anything.

Aquarius, 16-30°, Feminine, Negative, Magnetic

They are eccentric in some way, unpredictable, and independent. They also can be fearless.

Pisces, 0-15°, Feminine, Negative, Magnetic

They are easily influenced, self-sacrificing, brooding, and easily hurt, and some are dreamers or poets.

Pisces, 16-30°, Masculine, Positive, Electric

This position gives an influence of charity, and these people are also religious, mystical, sympathetic, and psychic.

Consider whether the sign on the cusp of a house is masculine or feminine and then consider what 15-degree section the sign is located in. If you want a finer look as to whether a man or woman (or both) will influence this house's affairs, it can be determined in this way.

The sign divided into two segments of 15 degrees each responds to number 2, and is more personally or emotionally oriented.

Dwads

The dwads identify with the twelve signs of the zodiac, and each sign has all twelve influences within the 30-degree sign. Each decanate has four dwads, or four quarters. Think of each decanate's dwads as similar to the four sections of the horoscope: east, north, west, south.

First Quarter (east): personality of self-image

Second Quarter (north): unconscious or inner self-image

Third Quarter (west): relating to a partner or others

Fourth Quarter (south): public image or success

Any system that uses four sections or four quarters of anything from the zodiac, horoscope, or sign has the above influence. The four dwads in each decanate also have these four influences. They also have all four of the elements of air, fire, water, earth within that decanate, which naturally has an additional elemental interpretation. This four quarters influence is associated with a more direct material influence of life. It is life itself as we know it (but not necessarily as it should be). It is more subjective and personal. It indicates how the person gets along with the sign itself, and the rulership of the quarter by sign and element are the tools the person has to work with. When thinking of a ruling quarter's element, it can influence the personality in connection with how it gets along with the element of the sign involved.

Navamsas

The navamsas have a Hindu origin. Each sign has nine divisions of 3⅓ degree each. The navamsas number 9 influence seems to respond and identify with the numerical evaluations combining numerological interpretations to the descriptions given below. They indicate a universal and more objective pattern for life.

The 3⅓ degree divisions indicate future possibilities and growth, and can show a potential of expression described by the sign which may not be always obvious. But most of all it seems to show the outcome of a situation as to the planet you are considering.

The nine sections of the navamsas of each sign seem to respond to the numbers 1 through 9. Use the same numerical influence as described at the beginning of this section, along with the descriptions that follow. The number descriptions will affect each section of nine in each sign.

Aries

0-3°20′; Aries ruled; Mars (Mars + Mars); No.1 vibration; energetic, impulsive activity

3°20′-6°40′; Taurus ruled; Venus (Venus + Mars); No.2 vibration; personal devotion, affectionate energy, a question of values

6°40'-10°; Gemini ruled; Mercury (Mercury + Mars); No.3 vibration; active mental energy

10°-13°20'; Cancer ruled; Moon (Moon + Mars); No.4 vibration; emotional energy or intensity of feelings

13°20'-16°40'; Leo ruled; Sun (Sun + Mars); No.5 vibration; vital energy and spontaneity (ego)

16°40'-20°; Virgo ruled; Mercury (Mercury + Mars); No.6 vibration; analytical mental energy, inner thoughts

20°-23°20'; Libra ruled; Venus (Venus + Mars); No.7 vibration; artistic energy or love with passion (very spiritual vibration)

23°20'-26°40'; Scorpio ruled; Mars, Pluto (Mars, Pluto + Mars); No.8 vibration; catalytic energy and healing potential

26°40'-30°; Sagittarius ruled; Jupiter (Jupiter + Mars); No.9 vibration; energy used to broadcast knowledge or unlimited energy

Taurus

0-3°20'; Capricorn ruled; Saturn (Saturn + Venus); No.1 vibration; controlled affections or a feeling of lack of love

3°20'-6°40'; Aquarius ruled; Uranus, Saturn (Uranus, Saturn + Venus); No.2 vibration; unconventional affections or unpredictable value system

6°40'-10°; Pisces ruled; Neptune, Jupiter (Neptune-Jupiter + Venus); No.3 vibration; spiritual or sacrificial affections or spiritual values

10°-13°20'; Aries ruled; Mars (Mars + Venus); No.4 vibration; erotic affections or energy in artistic works

13°20'-16°40'; Taurus ruled; Venus (Venus + Venus); No.5 vibration; love, artistry, true values, sensuousness

16°40'-20°; Gemini ruled; Mercury (Mercury + Venus); No.6 vibration; outward expression of love or love for a sibling

20°-23°20'; Cancer ruled; Moon (Moon + Venus); No.7 vibration; sentimental or family love (very spiritual influence)

23°20'-26°40'; Leo ruled; Sun (Sun + Venus); No. 8 vibration; personal love, magnetism and ego satisfaction

26°40'-30°; Virgo ruled; Mercury (Mercury + Venus); No.9 vibration; work done for loved ones, inward motivation

Gemini

0-3°20'; Libra ruled; Venus (Venus + Mercury); No.1 vibration; communication with a mate

3°20'-6°40'; Scorpio ruled; Mars, Pluto (Mars-Pluto + Mercury); No.2 vibration; mental activity and research leading to expression through speech or writing

6°40'-10°; Sagittarius ruled; Jupiter (Jupiter + Mercury); No.3 vibration; far-seeing, understanding

10°-13°20'; Capricorn ruled; Saturn (Saturn + Mercury); No.4 vibration; practical and serious, responsibility to a relative

13°20'-16°40'; Aquarius ruled; Uranus, Saturn (Uranus, Saturn + Mercury); No.5 vibration; ingenious and original

16°40'-20°; Pisces ruled; Neptune, Jupiter (Neptune, Jupiter + Mercury); No.6 vibration; poetic imagination, visionary and prophetic

20°-23°20'; Aries ruled; Mars (Mars + Mercury); No.7 vibration; quick-witted, quick temper

23°20'-26°40'; Taurus ruled; Venus (Venus + Mercury); No.8 vibration; cooperation with kindness, love for siblings, stubborn with angry domination (at times)

26°40'-30°; Gemini ruled; Mercury (Mercury + Mercury); No.9 vibration; mental flexibility, talent for writing

Cancer

0°-3:20'; Cancer ruled; Moon (Moon + Moon); No.1 vibration; sentimental regarding family and home

3°20'-6°40'; Leo ruled; Sun (Sun + Moon); No.2 vibration; basic characteristics integrated

6°40'-10°; Virgo ruled; Mercury (Mercury + Moon); No.3 vibration; responsive and aware of environment

10°-13°20'; Libra ruled; Venus (Venus + Moon); No.4 vibration; graceful and refined, responsive

13°20'-16°40'; Scorpio ruled; Mars, Pluto (Mars, Pluto + Moon); No.5 vibration; secretive with hidden depths

16°40'-20°; Sagittarius ruled; Jupiter (Jupiter + Moon); No.6 vibration; joyful and enthusiastic, understanding

20°-23°20'; Capricorn ruled; Saturn (Saturn + Moon); No.7 vibration (very spiritual); serious emotions, responsibility to family

23°20'-26°40'; Aquarius ruled; Uranus, Saturn (Uranus, Saturn + Moon); No.8 vibration; unusual and unpredictable with emotions

26°40'-30°; Pisces ruled; Neptune, Jupiter (Neptune, Jupiter + Moon); No.9 vibration; receptive and spiritual, visions

Leo

0°-3°20'; Aries ruled; Mars (Sun + Mars); No.1 vibration; demonstrative and energetic, fiery explosive

3°20'-6°40'; Taurus ruled; Venus (Venus + Sun); No.2 vibration; loving and noble, enjoyment of life

6°40'-10°; Gemini ruled; Mercury (Sun + Mercury); No.3 vibration; alert and attentive, glib in speaking and writing

10°-13°20'; Cancer ruled; Moon (Sun + Moon); No.4 vibration; confident and together

13°20'-16°40'; Leo ruled; Sun (Sun + Sun); No.5 vibration; ego adjusted and centered, fixed

16°40'-20°; Virgo ruled; Mercury (Mercury + Sun); No.6 vibration; analytical, intellectual pride

20°-23°20'; Libra ruled; Venus (Venus + Sun); No.7 vibration (very spiritual); elegant, in love with life

23o20-26o40; Scorpio ruled; Mars, Pluto (Mars, Pluto + Sun) No. 6 vibration; investigative, powerful; regenerative

26°40'-30°; Sagittarius ruled; Jupiter (Jupiter + Sun); No.9 vibration; generous and optimistic, expansive

Virgo

0°-3o20'; Capricorn ruled; Saturn (Saturn + Mercury); No.1 vibration; practical, systematic, serious, introspective

3°-6°40'; Aquarius ruled; Uranus, Saturn (Uranus, Saturn + Mercury); No.2 vibration; clever, brilliant, independent

6°40'-10°; Pisces ruled; Neptune, Jupiter (Neptune, Jupiter + Mercury); No.3 vibration; theorizing tendency, discriminating psychic talent

10°-13°20'; Aries ruled; Mars (Mars + Mercury); No.4 vibration; nervous energy, good worker

13°20'-16°40'; Taurus ruled; Venus (Venus + Mercury); No.5 vibration; loving service, money is important

16°40'-20°; Gemini ruled; Mercury (Mercury + Mercury); No.6 vibration; mentally agile, inner perception outwardly expressed

20°-23°20'; Cancer ruled; Moon (Moon + Mercury) No.7 vibration (very spiritual); emotional worry, service to family

23°20-26°40'; Leo ruled; Sun (Mercury + Sun); No.8 vibration; rational and alert

26°40'-30°; Virgo ruled; Mercury (Mercury + Mercury); No.9 vibration; analytical, nursing talent

Libra

0°-3°20'; Libra ruled; Venus (Venus + Venus); No.1 vibration; relating to others, artistic, diplomatic

3°20'-6°40'; Scorpio ruled; Mars, Pluto (Mars, Pluto + Venus); No.2 vibration; karmic love, fatalistic

6°40'-10°; Sagittarius ruled; Jupiter (Jupiter + Venus); No.3 vibration; lavish and exuberant with love, loving optimism

10°-13°20'; Capricorn ruled; Saturn (Saturn + Venus); No.4 vibration; caution in love, responsibility to loved ones

13°20'-16°40'; Aquarius ruled; Saturn, Uranus (Saturn, Uranus + Venus); No.5 vibration; unconventional and unpredictable in love

16°40'-20°; Pisces ruled; Jupiter, Neptune (Jupiter, Neptune + Venus); No.6 vibration; spiritual love with the ability to sacrifice, Artistically poetic

20°-23°20'; Aries ruled; Mars (Mars + Venus); No.7 vibration (very spiritual); amorous, love and passion together

23°20'-26°40'; Taurus ruled; Venus (Venus + Venus); No.8 vibration; love in a marital union, values—love and money

26°40'-30°; Gemini ruled; Mercury (Mercury + Venus); No.9 vibration; love for brothers and sisters, marriage and fulfilling communication

Scorpio

0°-3°20'; Cancer ruled; Moon (Moon + Mars, Pluto); No.1 vibration; emotional depth, karmic connection with family

3°20'-6°40'; Leo ruled; Sun (Sun + Mars, Pluto); No.2 vibrations; regenerative, powerful and strong

6°40'-10°; Virgo ruled; Mercury (Mercury + Mars, Pluto); No.3 vibration; secretive, investigative

10°-13°20'; Libra ruled; Venus (Venus + Mars, Pluto); No.4 vibration; compulsive love, love not understood

13°20'-16°40'; Scorpio ruled; Mars, Pluto (Mars, Pluto + Mars, Pluto); No.5 vibration; rebirth, lesson with death, healing power

16°40'-20°; Sagittarius ruled; Jupiter (Jupiter + Mars, Pluto); No.6 vibration; unseen resources, keen insight, investigative

20°-23°20'; Capricorn ruled; Saturn (Saturn + Mars, Pluto); No. 7 vibration (very spiritual influence); seclusive, ascetic, paternal influence

23°20'-26°40'; Aquarius ruled; Saturn, Uranus (Saturn, Uranus + Mars, Pluto); No.8 vibration; revolutionary experiences, karma with friendship

26°40'-30°; Pisces ruled; Jupiter, Neptune (Jupiter, Neptune + Mars, Pluto); No.9 vibration; ability to transcend the physical, out-of-body experiences

Sagittarius

0°-3°20′; Aries ruled; Mars (Mars + Jupiter); No.1 vibration; eager and enthusiastic, energy used for spiritual advancement

3°20′-6°40′; Taurus ruled; Venus (Venus + Jupiter); No.2 vibration; excessive, attracts resources, lucky with love

6°40′-10°; Gemini ruled; Mercury (Mercury + Jupiter) No.3 vibration; farseeing and prophetic, optimistic, expressive

10°-13°20′; Cancer ruled; Moon (Moon + Jupiter); No.4 vibration; fruitful, jovial, lucky with family, blessing in disguise

13°20′-16°40′; Leo ruled; Sun (Sun + Jupiter); No.5 vibration; happy, generous, outgoing

16°40′-20°; Virgo ruled; Mercury (Mercury + Jupiter); No.6 vibration; religious service, spiritual curiosity

20°-23°20′; Libra ruled; Venus (Venus + Jupiter); No.7 vibration (very spiritual); lucky in giving affections; happiness in love

23°20′-26°40′; Scorpio ruled; Mars, Pluto (Mars, Pluto + Jupiter); No.8 vibration; productive, over-extension of self

26°40′-30°; Sagittarius ruled; Jupiter (Jupiter + Jupiter); No.9 vibration; spiritual and moral outlook, optimistic and understanding

Capricorn

0°-3°20′; Capricorn ruled; Saturn (Saturn + Saturn); No.1 vibration; responsible and dutiful, ambitious with public success

3°20-6°40′; Aquarius ruled; Saturn, Uranus (Saturn, Uranus + Saturn); No.2 vibration; breaking free of restriction and/or being unique

6°40′-10°; Pisces ruled; Jupiter, Neptune (Jupiter, Neptune + Saturn); No.3 vibration; sacrifice required, ideal made workable, faith and reality

10°-13°20′; Aries ruled; Mars (Mars + Saturn); No.4 vibration; enduring, disciplined energy

13°20′-16°40′; Taurus ruled; Venus (Venus + Saturn); No.5 vibration; faithful, resourceful, work and money

16°40′-20°; Gemini ruled; Mercury (Mercury + Saturn); No.6 vibration; sensible knowledge disciplined study, responsibility to siblings

20°-23°20′; Cancer ruled; Moon (Moon + Saturn); No.7 vibration (very spiritual); restrained, disciplined emotions, duty to mother or family

23°20′-26°40′; Leo ruled; Sun (Sun + Saturn); No. 8 vibration; serious and realistic, reliable, dedicated love

26°40′-30°; Virgo ruled; Mercury (Mercury + Saturn); No.9 vibration; shrewd, detailed, practical

Aquarius

0°-3°20′; Libra ruled; Venus (Venus + Saturn, Uranus); No.1 vibration; unusual love, original art work

3°20′-6°40′; Scorpio ruled; Mars, Pluto (Mars, Pluto + Uranus, Saturn); No.2 vibration; reformer, catalyst

6°40′-10°; Sagittarius ruled; Jupiter (Jupiter + Uranus, Saturn); No.3 vibration; true humanitarian, understands human nature

10°-13°20′; Capricorn ruled; Saturn (Saturn + Saturn, Uranus); No.4 vibration; inventive

13°20′-16°40′; Aquarius ruled; Saturn, Uranus (Saturn, Uranus + Saturn, Uranus); No.5 vibration; scientific, original in manner, determined with independence

16°40′-20°; (Pisces ruled; Jupiter, Neptune (Jupiter, Neptune + Saturn, Uranus); No.5 vibration; altruistic, creative

20°-23°20′; Aries ruled; Mars (Mars + Saturn, Uranus); No.7 vibration (very spiritual influence); heroic, daring

23°20′-26°40′; Taurus ruled; Venus (Venus + Saturn, Uranus); No.8 vibration; true value is people, stubbornly independent

26°40′-30°; Gemini ruled; Mercury (Mercury + Saturn, Uranus); No.9 vibration; clever, original mind, possible severance from siblings

Pisces

0°-3°20′; Cancer ruled; Moon (Moon + Jupiter, Neptune); No.1 vibration; sympathetic, psychic, sacrificial feelings for family

3°20′-6°40′; Leo ruled; Sun (Sun + Jupiter, Neptune); No.2 vibration; idealistic, humble with ego, able to sacrifice for love

6°40′-10°; Virgo ruled; Mercury (Mercury + Jupiter, Neptune); No.3 vibration; poetic, visionary

10°-13°20′; Libra ruled; Venus (Venus + Jupiter, Neptune); No.4 vibration; tender, kind, musical

13°20′-16°40′; Scorpio ruled; Mars, Pluto (Mars, Pluto + Jupiter, Neptune); No.5 vibration; regenerative, mystical

16°40′-20°; Sagittarius ruled; Jupiter (Jupiter + Jupiter, Neptune); No.6 vibration; meditative, spiritual

20°-23°20′; Capricorn ruled; Saturn (Saturn + Jupiter, Neptune); No.7 vibration (very spiritual influence); pensive, ascetic, patience in confinement

23°20′-26°40′; Aquarius ruled; Saturn, Uranus (Saturn, Uranus + Jupiter, Neptune); No.8 vibration; obliging, unearthly, unconventional

26°40′-30°; Pisces ruled; Jupiter, Neptune (Jupiter, Neptune + Jupiter, Neptune); No.9 vibration; completion, true psychic, prophet

Now look to the house of the ruler of the navamsa to see a further outcome of a particular planet and situation in question. If there is more than one ruler of the navamsa (as with Aquarius-Saturn, Uranus) look to both houses. Both houses will influence the outcome.

Things to consider in interpreting the navamsas:

1. The sign.
2. The navamsa by sign and description.
3. Number vibration.
4. House position of the ruler of the navamsa.

www.ingramcontent.com/pod-product-compliance
Lightning Source LLC
Chambersburg PA
CBHW062106090426
42741CB00015B/3336